TEXES® 231 English Language Arts and Reading 7-12

Poppy U. Kennedy

This page is intentionally left blank.

This publication is not endorsed by any third-party organization. Names of exams are trademarks of respected organizations.

English Language Arts Learning

The text of this publication, or any part thereof, may not be reproduced in any manner whatsoever without written permission from English Language Arts Learning.

Printed in the United States of America

The authors, compilers, and publisher make no warranties regarding the correctness or completeness of the content contained in this publication and specifically disclaim all warranties whatsoever. Advice, strategies, and suggestions described may not be suitable for every case. Providing web addresses or other (information) services in this publication does not mean/imply that the author or publisher endorses information or websites. Neither the author nor the publisher shall be liable for damages arising herefrom. The author and publisher shall not be held responsible for any damage resulting herefrom from the information provided. There are no guarantees attached to the publication. The content of this publication is best practices, suggestions, common mistakes, and interpretation, and the author and the publisher are not responsible for any information contained in the publication.

**Disclaimer:** By using this book, you agree to the following: English Language Arts Learning and any individual/company/organization/group involved in the development of this publication specifically disclaims any liability (whether based on contract, tort, strict liability, or otherwise) for any direct, indirect, incidental, consequential, or special damages arising out of or in any way connected with access to the information presented in this publication, even if English Language Arts Learning and any individual/company/organization/group involved in the development of this publication have been advised of the possibility of such damages.

English Language Arts Learning and any individual/company/organization/group involved in the development of this publication are not responsible for the use of this information. Information provided through this publication holds no warranty of accuracy, correctness, or truth. The author, publisher, compilers, and all other parties involved in this work disclaim all responsibility for any errors contained within this work and from the results of the use of this information.

**No individual or institution has permission to reproduce (in any form) the contents of this publication.**

**No individual or institution has permission to reproduce the contents on any website.**

This page is intentionally left blank.

## Table of Content

Chapter 1 – Questions .................................................................................................................... 1

Chapter 2 – Answers and Explanations ....................................................................................... 41

This page is intentionally left blank.

# Chapter 1 – Questions

## QUESTION 1

In which genre do authors primarily use dialogue and stage directions to convey the story?

- A. Fiction
- B. Drama
- C. Poetry
- D. Young adult literary texts

## QUESTION 2

Which of the following best illustrates the connotative meaning of the word "home"?

- A. A physical structure where a person lives.
- B. A place of warmth, comfort, and belonging.
- C. A synonym for "residence."
- D. An antonym for "house."

## QUESTION 3

What aspect of the English language is influenced by regional factors?

- A. Syntactic rules
- B. Word structure
- C. Homonyms
- D. Dialects

## QUESTION 4

In an informational text about climate change, which of the following statements represents the main idea of the text?

- A. The impact of climate change on polar bears.
- B. The causes of global warming.
- C. Strategies for reducing greenhouse gas emissions.
- D. The urgency of addressing climate change for future generations.

## QUESTION 5

"In the dystopian world of George Orwell's '1984,' the omnipresent government surveillance serves as a symbol of control and oppression. The all-seeing Big Brother, with his slogan 'War is Peace, Freedom is Slavery, Ignorance is Strength,' manipulates not only the physical world but also the minds of the citizens. The telescreens that are ubiquitous in this society represent a constant intrusion into the private lives of the people, fostering an atmosphere of fear and self-censorship."

In the provided excerpt, what literary device is exemplified by the slogan "War is Peace, Freedom is Slavery, Ignorance is Strength" in George Orwell's '1984'?

- A. Foreshadowing.
- B. Allusion.
- C. Oxymoron.
- D. Hyperbole.

QUESTION 6

Which genre often utilizes rhyme, rhythm, and various poetic devices to express emotions and ideas?

- A. Fiction
- B. Drama
- C. Poetry
- D. Young adult literary texts

QUESTION 7

The myth of the Minotaur is associated with which region's literature?

- A. Africa
- B. Asia
- C. Latin America
- D. Europe

QUESTION 8

Which literary device is used when an author exaggerates to emphasize a point or create a humorous effect?

- A. Simile
- B. Metaphor
- C. Hyperbole
- D. Personification

QUESTION 9

Which word is a derivative of the Latin word "amare" meaning "to love"?

- A. Amiable
- B. Ambivalent
- C. Amorous
- D. Anxious

QUESTION 10

What historical influence significantly contributed to the development of the English language, particularly in terms of vocabulary?

- A. The Renaissance
- B. The Industrial Revolution
- C. The Space Age
- D. The Victorian Era

QUESTION 11

Which of the following words is an antonym for "benevolent"?

- A. Malevolent
- B. Ambivalent
- C. Altruistic
- D. Cordial

## QUESTION 12

Which term refers to the overall message or main idea conveyed in a literary work?

A. Theme
B. Conflict
C. Symbolism
D. Imagery

## QUESTION 13

Which skill involves comparing and contrasting how different texts address similar themes or subjects?

A. Interpreting word choices
B. Analyzing text structure
C. Determining central ideas
D. Analyzing similar themes or topics

## QUESTION 14

In which way do authors draw on prior literary texts to create their own original works?

A. By replicating the entire plot
B. By incorporating well-known characters
C. By transforming existing texts
D. By disregarding all prior literary traditions

## QUESTION 15

What is the intended audience for an informational text about advanced astrophysics theories?

A. Elementary school students
B. College professors and researchers
C. General science enthusiasts
D. Professional chefs

## QUESTION 16

Which of the following statements from an informational text about the solar system is a specific detail rather than a general statement?

A. "The solar system consists of eight planets."
B. "Mars is known as the 'Red Planet' due to its reddish appearance."
C. "The sun is at the center of the solar system."
D. "Planets in the solar system orbit around the sun."

## QUESTION 17

Which aspect of text structure focuses on the relationship between sentences, paragraphs, and the overall text?

A. Figurative language
B. Point of view
C. Word choice
D. Text coherence

## QUESTION 18

What does it mean to interpret words and phrases in a literary text?

- A. Analyze the author's biography
- B. Examine the grammatical structure
- C. Identify the genre of the text
- D. Understand the figurative and connotative meanings

## QUESTION 19

Which element of literary analysis involves examining the impact of specific word choices on a text's overall meaning, tone, and mood?

- A. Theme analysis
- B. Character development
- C. Plot structure
- D. Word choice analysis

## QUESTION 20

In which genre are fictional stories created using imaginative elements and often feature plot, characters, and settings?

- A. Fiction
- B. Drama
- C. Poetry
- D. Young adult literary texts

## QUESTION 21

Which genre commonly employs acts, scenes, and dramatic conventions to present its narrative?

- A. Fiction
- B. Drama
- C. Poetry
- D. Young adult literary texts

## QUESTION 22

What literary element refers to the recurring patterns of stressed and unstressed syllables in a line of poetry?

- A. Alliteration
- B. Onomatopoeia
- C. Meter
- D. Symbolism

## QUESTION 23

Which skill involves examining how specific sentences, paragraphs, or sections of a text contribute to its overall structure and meaning?

- A. Analyzing point of view
- B. Analyzing figurative language
- C. Analyzing text structure
- D. Analyzing character development

## QUESTION 24

"In Shakespeare's play 'Hamlet,' the character Hamlet grapples with profound existential questions about the nature of life and death. In Act III, Scene I, he famously delivers the soliloquy: 'To be or not to be, that is the question: Whether 'tis nobler in the mind to suffer The slings and arrows of outrageous fortune, Or to take arms against a sea of troubles And, by opposing, end them.' This introspective contemplation reflects Hamlet's internal struggle as he ponders the moral and philosophical implications of existence."

In the provided excerpt from 'Hamlet,' which literary device is exemplified by the line "To be or not to be, that is the question"?

A. Metaphor.
B. Irony.
C. Alliteration.
D. Antithesis.

## QUESTION 25

What is the primary purpose of analyzing the impact of specific word choices on a literary text?

A. To identify the genre of the text
B. To analyze the plot structure
C. To determine the author's biographical information
D. To understand the text's meaning, tone, and mood

## QUESTION 26

In a high school English class, a student asks the teacher to explain the concept of theme in a literary text. Which response best explains the concept to the student?

A. "Theme refers to the genre or category of the literary text, such as fiction, drama, or poetry."
B. "Theme represents the overall message or central idea explored in a literary work, providing deeper insights into its meaning and purpose."
C. "Theme refers to the use of figurative language and poetic devices in a literary text to create vivid imagery and sensory experiences for the reader."
D. "Theme involves analyzing the grammatical structure and sentence patterns in a literary text to understand the author's style and writing techniques."

## QUESTION 27

A high school English teacher wants to analyze how two different texts treat similar themes of social inequality. Which approach would be most effective?

A. Comparing the settings and characters of the two texts to identify similarities and differences in their portrayals of social inequality.
B. Focusing on the different genres of the two texts and how they impact the exploration of social inequality.
C. Analyzing the authors' biographical information to understand their personal perspectives on social inequality.
D. Examining the historical context in which the two texts were written to gain insights into the societal issues they address.

## QUESTION 28

What is typically the intended audience for a persuasive speech advocating for stricter gun control laws?

A. Firearms enthusiasts
B. Elementary school children
C. Law enforcement officers
D. The general public and policymakers

## QUESTION 29

In a persuasive article arguing for increased funding for public schools, what is the author's likely point of view?

- A. That public schools are already adequately funded
- B. That funding for public schools should be reduced
- C. That increased funding is essential for improving public education
- D. That private schools are superior to public schools

## QUESTION 30

A literature professor wants to analyze how an author draws on and transforms prior literary texts and traditions to develop an original work. Which aspect should the professor focus on?

- A. Identifying direct quotations or references to other literary texts in the author's work.
- B. Examining the historical context in which the author's work was written to understand its influences.
- C. Analyzing how the author incorporates and modifies themes, characters, or storylines from previous texts.
- D. Investigating the author's personal motivations and experiences that shaped their creative process.

## QUESTION 31

A student is analyzing a poem and wants to understand the impact of specific word choices on the poem's meaning, tone, and mood. What should the student focus on?

- A. The historical context in which the poem was written and the social issues it addresses.
- B. The author's biographical information and personal experiences that influenced the poem.
- C. The figurative language, such as metaphors or similes, used in the poem.
- D. The grammatical structure and sentence patterns employed in the poem.

## QUESTION 32

A high school English teacher is analyzing the structure of a novel and wants to examine how specific sentences and paragraphs relate to each other and contribute to the overall text. Which approach would be most effective?

- A. Analyzing the use of dialogue and its impact on character development and plot progression.
- B. Identifying the main conflict and its resolution throughout the novel.
- C. Tracing the development of a specific theme or motif through the novel.
- D. Examining the transitions and connections between sentences and paragraphs in the novel.

## QUESTION 33

During which period did the epic poem "Beowulf" originate?

- A. Anglo-Saxon and Middle Ages
- B. English Renaissance
- C. Victorian
- D. Contemporary

## QUESTION 34

What is the central idea of a persuasive advertisement for a new electric car model?

- A. The benefits of public transportation
- B. The history of fossil fuel usage
- C. The advantages of owning an electric car
- D. The importance of reducing carbon emissions

## QUESTION 35

In a piece of propaganda aimed at influencing public opinion during a political campaign, what is a common characteristic?

- A. Providing balanced and unbiased information
- B. Offering a range of policy options for consideration
- C. Using emotional appeals and one-sided arguments
- D. Focusing on historical facts and analysis

## QUESTION 36

Which period in British literature is often associated with the works of William Shakespeare?

- A. Elizabethan
- B. Romantic
- C. Restoration/Enlightenment
- D. Modern

## QUESTION 37

What is a common characteristic of technical texts, such as warranties and contracts?

- A. Providing creative and imaginative storytelling
- B. Offering a range of emotional appeals
- C. Using specialized language and legal terms
- D. Focusing on personal anecdotes and experiences

## QUESTION 38

In a warranty document for a consumer product, what is the primary purpose?

- A. To entertain and engage the reader
- B. To inform the reader about the product's history
- C. To outline the terms and conditions of product coverage
- D. To share customer reviews and testimonials

## QUESTION 39

The novel "Jane Eyre" by Charlotte Brontë belongs to which period?

- A. Victorian
- B. Modern
- C. English Renaissance
- D. Postcolonial

## QUESTION 40

The play "Waiting for Godot" by Samuel Beckett is associated with which period in British literature?

- A. Modern
- B. Anglo-Saxon and Middle Ages
- C. Restoration/Enlightenment
- D. Romantic

## QUESTION 41

Which period in British literature is associated with the rise of the British Empire and its influence on literature?

- A. Postcolonial
- B. Victorian
- C. English Renaissance
- D. Romantic

## QUESTION 42

The novel "Pride and Prejudice" by Jane Austen is set in which period of British literature?

- A. English Renaissance
- B. Victorian
- C. Restoration/Enlightenment
- D. Romantic

## QUESTION 43

Which period in British literature is known for its emphasis on reason, logic, and scientific advancements?

- A. Restoration/Enlightenment
- B. Postcolonial
- C. Anglo-Saxon and Middle Ages
- D. Modern

## QUESTION 44

The novel "Frankenstein" by Mary Shelley is associated with which period in British literature?

- A. Romantic
- B. Victorian
- C. Modern
- D. Anglo-Saxon and Middle Ages

## QUESTION 45

When analyzing a persuasive text for logical fallacies, which of the following fallacies involves making a personal attack against the opponent rather than addressing the argument itself?

- A. Ad hominem.
- B. Red herring.
- C. Slippery slope.
- D. Hasty generalization.

## QUESTION 46

In a persuasive text, what is the purpose of employing a "call to action"?

- A. To provide historical context.
- B. To present opposing viewpoints.
- C. To encourage readers to take a specific action.
- D. To include vivid sensory details.

## QUESTION 47

Which period in British literature is known for its focus on social realism, industrialization, and class divisions?

- A. Victorian
- B. English Renaissance
- C. Contemporary
- D. Postcolonial

## QUESTION 48

The poetry of T.S. Eliot is associated with which period in British literature?

- A. Modern
- B. Romantic
- C. Anglo-Saxon and Middle Ages
- D. Restoration/Enlightenment

## QUESTION 49

In narrative writing, what is the purpose of using the "in medias res" approach?

- A. To provide a detailed background on the main characters
- B. To start the story with the climax or a critical moment
- C. To include multiple flashbacks to different time periods
- D. To emphasize the significance of minor events

## QUESTION 50

What is the primary purpose of citing or acknowledging sources appropriately in a text?

- A. To make your writing seem more authoritative.
- B. To give credit to the original authors and avoid plagiarism.
- C. To demonstrate your personal knowledge of the topic.
- D. To create a sense of mystery about your sources.

## QUESTION 51

Which of the following is a method for appropriately acknowledging a source in an academic text?

- A. Including the source information in the conclusion of the paper.
- B. Listing the source in a separate document.
- C. Using in-text citations and providing a bibliography.
- D. Mentioning the source verbally in a presentation.

## QUESTION 52

Which period in British literature is associated with the decline of feudalism and the rise of the middle class?

- A. Restoration/Enlightenment
- B. Anglo-Saxon and Middle Ages
- C. English Renaissance
- D. Postcolonial

## QUESTION 53

The play "An Inspector Calls" by J.B. Priestley reflects the social concerns of which period in British literature?

A. Modern
B. Victorian
C. Postcolonial
D. Romantic

## QUESTION 54

Which period in British literature is characterized by the exploration of postmodern themes, metafiction, and intertextuality?

A. Contemporary
B. Victorian
C. Romantic
D. Restoration/Enlightenment

## QUESTION 55

Which theory of language acquisition emphasizes the role of innate, universal grammar in language development?

A. Behaviorism
B. Interactionist
C. Social-cultural
D. Generative

## QUESTION 56

Which reading strategy involves making predictions about the content of a text based on prior knowledge and text clues?

A. Summarizing
B. Visualizing
C. Inferring
D. Questioning

## QUESTION 57

Which component of language-based reading disabilities is characterized by difficulty in accurately and fluently recognizing words?

A. Phonological processing
B. Comprehension
C. Vocabulary
D. Syntax

## QUESTION 58

Which approach to second-language instruction emphasizes the use of the target language for meaningful communication from the beginning?

A. Grammar-translation
B. Audio-lingual
C. Communicative language teaching
D. Content-based instruction

## QUESTION 59

Which comprehension strategy involves actively monitoring one's understanding of the text while reading?

- A. Predicting
- B. Visualizing
- C. Questioning
- D. Monitoring

## QUESTION 60

Which technique is used to establish the significance of a claim and differentiate it from opposing claims?

- A. Rhetorical question
- B. Counterargument
- C. Anecdote
- D. Statistical evidence

## QUESTION 61

Which element of an argumentative essay is responsible for logically organizing claims, counterclaims, reasons, and evidence?

- A. Thesis statement
- B. Introduction
- C. Conclusion
- D. Body paragraphs

## QUESTION 62

"Virginia Woolf's 'To the Lighthouse' is a masterpiece of modernist literature. Set in the early 20th century, the novel explores the inner thoughts and perceptions of its characters, using stream-of-consciousness narrative techniques. In one of the pivotal scenes, the character Lily Briscoe grapples with her artistic ambitions and the challenges of representing truth in her paintings. Woolf's intricate prose delves into the complexities of human consciousness and the elusive nature of reality."

In the provided excerpt about 'To the Lighthouse,' what literary movement is exemplified by the novel's use of stream-of-consciousness narrative techniques?

- A. Realism, a literary movement characterized by the depiction of everyday life and ordinary people.
- B. Romanticism, a literary movement that emphasizes emotion, nature, and individualism.
- C. Modernism, a literary movement known for its experimental narrative techniques and exploration of inner thoughts.
- D. Naturalism, a literary movement that focuses on deterministic forces and the impact of environment on characters.

## QUESTION 63

What is the main purpose of an informational text about healthy eating habits?

- A. To promote a specific diet plan
- B. To inform readers about the benefits of exercise
- C. To educate people about making nutritious food choices
- D. To share personal anecdotes about the author's eating habits

## QUESTION 64

Which writing technique is used to create cohesion and clarify relationships between different parts of an argumentative text?

- A. Simile
- B. Metaphor
- C. Transition words
- D. Hyperbole

## QUESTION 65

When developing claims and counterclaims in an argumentative essay, what should writers consider in terms of evidence?

- A. Including all available evidence
- B. Focusing on evidence that supports their own claims
- C. Providing relevant evidence for both claims and counterclaims
- D. Ignoring evidence that weakens their own claims

## QUESTION 66

What is the purpose of a concluding statement or section in an argumentative essay?

- A. To introduce a new claim
- B. To summarize the entire essay
- C. To restate the thesis statement
- D. To support and follow from the argument presented

## QUESTION 67

In an informational text about the history of the internet, which of the following statements represents a general statement about the topic?

- A. "Tim Berners-Lee invented the World Wide Web in 1989."
- B. "The ARPANET project laid the foundation for the modern internet."
- C. "Online communication and information sharing have transformed society."
- D. "The internet has had a profound impact on various industries."

## QUESTION 68

Which narrative technique involves revealing information about a character's thoughts, feelings, and motivations?

- A. Dialogue
- B. Pacing
- C. Description
- D. Reflection

## QUESTION 69

Which element of narrative writing engages the reader by presenting a problem, situation, or observation and its significance?

- A. Point of view
- B. Setting
- C. Conflict
- D. Orientation

## QUESTION 70

What is a typical characteristic of functional texts, such as timetables and application forms?

- A. Providing detailed narratives and stories
- B. Using persuasive language to convince readers
- C. Presenting information in a clear and organized format
- D. Sharing personal opinions and preferences

## QUESTION 71

When reading a consumer contract, what can consumers gain knowledge about?

A. The company's marketing strategies
B. The product's popularity in the market
C. Their rights and responsibilities as consumers
D. The CEO's personal experiences with the product

## QUESTION 72

Which technique refers to the strategic use of visual aids, such as charts, graphs, images, or videos, to enhance audience understanding and engagement during a presentation?

A. Ethos
B. Pathos
C. Logos
D. Multimedia

## QUESTION 73

Which technique is used to create a coherent narrative by sequencing events that build on one another?

A. Flashback
B. Foreshadowing
C. Chronological order
D. In medias res

## QUESTION 74

Which narrative technique adds depth and complexity to a story by incorporating multiple plot lines or story threads?

A. Foil characters
B. Subplots
C. Red herrings
D. Parallel structure

## QUESTION 75

Which element of narrative writing helps convey a vivid picture of experiences, events, setting, and characters?

A. Figurative language
B. Foreshadowing
C. Conflict
D. Climax

## QUESTION 76

Which technique combines informative and explanatory writing within a narrative?

A. Flashback
B. Foreshadowing
C. Exposition
D. Stream of consciousness

## QUESTION 77

Which element of narrative writing provides a sense of resolution and reflects on what has been experienced or observed?

- A. Climax
- B. Falling action
- C. Denouement
- D. Rising action

## QUESTION 78

Which narrative technique involves the use of characters' direct speech?

- A. Dialogue
- B. Description
- C. Reflection
- D. Monologue

## QUESTION 79

What is the primary purpose of a timetable for a public transportation system?

- A. To advertise local tourist attractions
- B. To share customer feedback and testimonials
- C. To provide clear information on departure and arrival times
- D. To promote discounts and special offers

## QUESTION 80

Which technique is used to build toward a particular tone or outcome in a narrative?

- A. Symbolism
- B. Foreshadowing
- C. Flashback
- D. Stream of consciousness

## QUESTION 81

Which of the following literary works is associated with ancient Africa?

- A. "Things Fall Apart" by Chinua Achebe
- B. "One Hundred Years of Solitude" by Gabriel Garcia Marquez
- C. "The Odyssey" by Homer
- D. "The Divine Comedy" by Dante Alighieri

## QUESTION 82

Which literary form is commonly associated with Asian literature?

- A. Haiku
- B. Sonnet
- C. Epic poem
- D. Gothic novel

## QUESTION 83

The novel "One Hundred Years of Solitude" is an example of literature from which region?

- A. Africa
- B. Asia
- C. Latin America
- D. Europe

## QUESTION 84

Which of the following works is a classic of Caribbean literature?

- A. "The Count of Monte Cristo" by Alexandre Dumas
- B. "Wide Sargasso Sea" by Jean Rhys
- C. "Don Quixote" by Miguel de Cervantes
- D. "Pride and Prejudice" by Jane Austen

## QUESTION 85

The play "Hamlet" by William Shakespeare originated from which region?

- A. Africa
- B. Asia
- C. Latin America
- D. Europe

## QUESTION 86

Which of the following religious texts is associated with Asian literature?

- A. "The Bhagavad Gita"
- B. "The Canterbury Tales"
- C. "Paradise Lost"
- D. "The Aeneid"

## QUESTION 87

When selecting and limiting a subject for narrative writing, what should writers consider?

- A. Including every possible detail to make the story comprehensive
- B. Focusing solely on personal experiences without any broader themes
- C. Choosing a specific aspect or moment that best conveys the intended message
- D. Avoiding any use of personal anecdotes or reflections

## QUESTION 88

In a narrative essay describing a memorable vacation, which of the following would be a relevant detail to include?

- A. A detailed analysis of weather patterns during the trip
- B. The writer's favorite restaurant in their hometown
- C. An anecdote about an unexpected adventure during the vacation
- D. The writer's plans for future vacations

QUESTION 89

What is the primary purpose of narrative writing?

- A. To persuade the reader to take a specific action
- B. To provide a detailed analysis of a complex issue
- C. To entertain and engage the reader with a story or personal experience
- D. To present factual information in a straightforward manner

QUESTION 90

"In F. Scott Fitzgerald's 'The Great Gatsby,' the character of Jay Gatsby embodies the American Dream and its elusive nature. Gatsby's opulent mansion, lavish parties, and relentless pursuit of wealth are symbols of his aspiration to attain the American Dream. However, beneath this façade lies a complex character yearning for the unattainable: his lost love, Daisy Buchanan. Fitzgerald's novel explores the themes of wealth, excess, and the emptiness that can accompany the pursuit of the American Dream in the Jazz Age."

In the provided excerpt from 'The Great Gatsby,' what literary device is used when describing Gatsby's mansion, parties, and pursuit of wealth as symbols of his aspiration to attain the American Dream?

- A. Symbolism, a literary device where objects, characters, or events represent deeper meanings or ideas.
- B. Allegory, a literary device where characters or events represent abstract concepts or moral qualities.
- C. Irony, a literary device that involves a contradiction between appearance and reality.
- D. Foreshadowing, a literary device that hints at future events in the narrative.

QUESTION 91

Which author is known for his/her contribution to Latin American literature?

- A. Rabindranath Tagore
- B. Pablo Neruda
- C. Fyodor Dostoevsky
- D. Virginia Woolf

QUESTION 92

The novel "Madame Bovary" was written by an author from which region?

- A. Africa
- B. Asia
- C. Latin America
- D. Europe

QUESTION 93

The Caribbean author Derek Walcott is associated with which literary form?

- A. Epic poem
- B. Short story
- C. Drama
- D. Satirical novel

QUESTION 94

Which of the following works represents the Gothic genre in European literature?

- A. "Things Fall Apart" by Chinua Achebe
- B. "The Kite Runner" by Khaled Hosseini
- C. "Dracula" by Bram Stoker
- D. "To Kill a Mockingbird" by Harper Lee

## QUESTION 95

Which of the following statements accurately reflects the influence of technology on the development of Standard American English?

- A. Technology has had minimal impact on the development of Standard American English.
- B. Technology has led to the decline of Standard American English.
- C. Technology has facilitated the rapid evolution and spread of Standard American English.
- D. Technology has resulted in the stagnation of Standard American English.

## QUESTION 96

When encountering an unfamiliar word, which of the following strategies would be most effective in determining its meaning?

- A. Relying solely on contextual clues within the sentence.
- B. Consulting a thesaurus for synonyms of the unknown word.
- C. Conducting a thorough etymological analysis of the word's origins.
- D. Identifying and analyzing the word's morphological components.

## QUESTION 97

Which of the following best describes the distinction between general academic and domain-specific vocabulary?

- A. General academic vocabulary refers to words used in everyday conversation, while domain-specific vocabulary is limited to specialized fields.
- B. General academic vocabulary encompasses a wide range of subjects, while domain-specific vocabulary is limited to a particular discipline or profession.
- C. General academic vocabulary is standardized across all disciplines, while domain-specific vocabulary varies significantly.
- D. General academic vocabulary primarily consists of technical terms, while domain-specific vocabulary consists of common words and phrases.

## QUESTION 98

Which of the following techniques is most effective for vocabulary acquisition through context and word study?

- A. Memorizing lists of isolated vocabulary words.
- B. Utilizing flashcards to practice word recognition.
- C. Engaging in extensive reading and encountering words in meaningful contexts.
- D. Focusing solely on the analysis of word roots and affixes.

## QUESTION 99

What is a common barrier to listening effectively in interpersonal communication?

- A. Demonstrating empathy and active engagement
- B. Making eye contact with the speaker
- C. Preconceived judgments and biases
- D. Responding with thoughtful questions

## QUESTION 100

In a group discussion, what is a method of active participation that involves rephrasing what someone has said to ensure understanding?

- A. Interrupting to share one's own perspective
- B. Offering unsolicited advice
- C. Restating or paraphrasing the speaker's points
- D. Remaining silent to avoid conflicts

## QUESTION 101

Which of the following statements best illustrates the distinction between denotative and connotative meanings of words?

- A. The denotative meaning of "home" is a place where someone lives, while its connotative meaning evokes a sense of warmth and belonging.
- B. Denotative and connotative meanings of words are interchangeable and can be used interchangeably in all contexts.
- C. The denotative meaning of a word is subjective and varies from person to person, while the connotative meaning is objective and universally understood.
- D. Denotative meanings of words are associated with emotions and personal experiences, while connotative meanings are factual and dictionary-based.

## QUESTION 102

Which rhetorical strategy is used when a writer acknowledges and addresses counterarguments in order to strengthen their own argument?

- A. Ethos
- B. Pathos
- C. Logos
- D. Refutation

## QUESTION 103

Which of the following best describes the role of cultural factors in spoken and written communication?

- A. Cultural factors have no influence on spoken and written communication.
- B. Cultural factors affect only written communication, not spoken communication.
- C. Cultural factors impact both spoken and written communication, shaping language use and interpretation.
- D. Cultural factors primarily influence spoken communication, but have minimal impact on written communication.

## QUESTION 104

Which of the following strategies is most effective for writing effectively for a variety of audiences, purposes, and contexts?

- A. Using complex vocabulary and specialized terminology to demonstrate expertise.
- B. Adopting a formal and rigid writing style to maintain professionalism.
- C. Adapting the tone, style, and language to suit the specific audience, purpose, and context.
- D. Focusing solely on personal opinions and experiences to engage the reader emotionally.

## QUESTION 105

Which stage of the writing process involves reviewing and improving the overall organization, coherence, and effectiveness of a written text?

- A. Planning
- B. Drafting
- C. Revising
- D. Editing

## QUESTION 106

Which of the following strategies is most effective for editing written texts to achieve conformity with conventions of Standard English usage?

- A. Relying solely on grammar and spell-checking software for error detection.
- B. Consulting a thesaurus to find synonyms for commonly used words.
- C. Engaging in peer editing or seeking feedback from knowledgeable individuals.
- D. Ignoring minor errors and focusing only on the overall content and ideas.

## QUESTION 107

Which of the following elements is most appropriate to use when developing a conclusion that follows from and supports the information or explanation presented in an informational or explanatory text?

- A. Introducing new ideas or topics unrelated to the main content.
- B. Restating the introduction verbatim to create cohesion.
- C. Summarizing the main points and providing a final thought or insight.
- D. Ending abruptly without providing a concluding statement.

## QUESTION 108

Which of the following is an effective way to use precise language and domain-specific vocabulary when informing or explaining a topic?

- A. Overloading the text with technical jargon and terminology.
- B. Avoiding specific terms and using general language to cater to a wider audience.
- C. Balancing the use of domain-specific vocabulary with explanations or definitions for clarity.
- D. Using figurative language and metaphors to enhance the reader's understanding.

## QUESTION 109

Which of the following is a key function of appropriate and varied transitions in an informational or explanatory text?

- A. To confuse the reader and create ambiguity.
- B. To provide a chronological account of events or information.
- C. To link the major sections of the text and create cohesion.
- D. To introduce unrelated ideas and concepts.

## QUESTION 110

Which of the following is an example of using a literary device to affect meaning in an informational or explanatory text?

- A. Using vivid sensory details to describe a scene.
- B. Incorporating dialogue between characters.
- C. Employing irony to create a humorous tone.
- D. Using figurative language to convey emotions.

## QUESTION 111

Which of the following techniques is most effective for developing a research question and narrowing or broadening inquiry as appropriate?

- A. Stating a general topic without considering specific research objectives.
- B. Conducting preliminary research before developing a focused research question.
- C. Limiting inquiry to a single perspective or point of view.
- D. Adopting a fixed research question without flexibility for adjustments.

## QUESTION 112

Which of the following techniques is most appropriate for assessing the strengths and limitations of prospective sources in terms of task, purpose, audience, and credibility?

- A. Relying solely on popular sources that have a large readership.
- B. Considering the author's personal background and experiences.
- C. Evaluating the currency, relevance, and reliability of the source.
- D. Assessing the visual appeal and design of the source material.

QUESTION 113

Which of the following techniques is most effective for integrating information into a text selectively to maintain the development of ideas while avoiding plagiarism and overreliance on any one source?

- A. Copying and pasting large portions of text from a single source.
- B. Paraphrasing extensively without proper citation.
- C. Quoting directly from multiple sources and providing proper citations.
- D. Excluding all external sources to rely solely on personal knowledge.

QUESTION 114

Which of the following techniques is most important for citing material accurately using a standard format?

- A. Including citations only for direct quotations, not for paraphrased information.
- B. Using any citation format as long as it is consistent throughout the text.
- C. Consulting a variety of citation style guides and selecting the one that is most convenient.
- D. Adhering to a specific citation style guide recommended by the academic or publishing institution.

QUESTION 115

What is the primary purpose of using nonverbal cues in conversations?

- A. To provide a written record of the conversation
- B. To emphasize the importance of the topic
- C. To express feelings, emotions, and intentions
- D. To encourage interruptions and side discussions

QUESTION 116

Which of the following techniques is most effective for presenting information by using structure and style appropriate to the task, purpose, and audience?

- A. Utilizing complex and technical language to demonstrate expertise.
- B. Using a casual and conversational tone to connect with the audience.
- C. Adapting the structure and style to suit the specific requirements and expectations.
- D. Including personal anecdotes and unrelated tangents to engage the reader.

QUESTION 117

Which literary movement in American literature emerged in the mid-19th century and emphasized intuition, imagination, and nature?

- A. Realism
- B. Transcendentalism
- C. Naturalism
- D. Romanticism

QUESTION 118

Which American literary work is a representative example of the Harlem Renaissance, an artistic and intellectual movement of the 1920s?

- A. "The Catcher in the Rye" by J.D. Salinger
- B. "The Great Gatsby" by F. Scott Fitzgerald
- C. "Their Eyes Were Watching God" by Zora Neale Hurston
- D. "Moby-Dick" by Herman Melville

QUESTION 119

Which literary period in American literature was characterized by a rejection of societal norms, experimentation with language and form, and disillusionment with traditional values?

- A. Romanticism
- B. Realism
- C. Modernism
- D. Transcendentalism

QUESTION 120

Which American author is associated with the Beat Generation, a literary movement that emerged in the 1950s and emphasized nonconformity, spirituality, and spontaneous writing?

- A. Jack Kerouac
- B. F. Scott Fitzgerald
- C. Ernest Hemingway
- D. Mark Twain

QUESTION 121

Which American poet is known for his/her unconventional use of punctuation, capitalization, and syntax, challenging traditional poetic norms?

- A. Robert Frost
- B. Emily Dickinson
- C. Langston Hughes
- D. e.e. cummings

QUESTION 122

Which literary genre is characterized by exaggerated characters, humorous situations, and satirical social commentary?

- A. Gothic fiction
- B. Realistic fiction
- C. Satire
- D. Science fiction

QUESTION 123

Which American literary work is an example of postmodern literature that challenges traditional narrative structures and blurs the line between reality and fiction?

- A. "The Grapes of Wrath" by John Steinbeck
- B. "Beloved" by Toni Morrison
- C. "House of Leaves" by Mark Z. Danielewski
- D. "To Kill a Mockingbird" by Harper Lee

QUESTION 124

Which element of visual images in media refers to the arrangement of visual elements, such as color, shapes, and objects, within the frame?

- A. Themes
- B. Filters
- C. Composition
- D. Aesthetics

## QUESTION 125

What is the term for the practice of altering visual images in media to influence public opinion or change personal behavior?

- A. Aesthetics
- B. Filters
- C. Manipulation
- D. Themes

## QUESTION 126

How can personal experience and prior knowledge impact an individual's interpretation of visual images in media?

- A. They have no effect on interpretation.
- B. They provide a universal interpretation.
- C. They can influence perception and meaning.
- D. They always lead to a biased interpretation.

## QUESTION 127

Which American author's works often address themes of social inequality, racism, and the effects of colonialism?

- A. William Faulkner
- B. Ralph Ellison
- C. Zora Neale Hurston
- D. Toni Morrison

## QUESTION 128

Which American literary movement emerged in the late 20th century and is characterized by a focus on personal experiences, identity, and the challenges faced by marginalized communities?

- A. Transcendentalism
- B. Postcolonialism
- C. Magical realism
- D. Ethnic literature

## QUESTION 129

Which American playwright is associated with the Theater of the Absurd, a movement that presents a fragmented, illogical, and absurd portrayal of the human condition?

- A. Tennessee Williams
- B. Arthur Miller
- C. Samuel Beckett
- D. August Wilson

## QUESTION 130

Which American literary work is an example of regionalism, a movement that focused on depicting specific regions and local customs in detail?

- A. "The Scarlet Letter" by Nathaniel Hawthorne
- B. "The Adventures of Tom Sawyer" by Mark Twain
- C. "The Sun Also Rises" by Ernest Hemingway
- D. "Moby-Dick" by Herman Melville

## QUESTION 131

Which American poet is associated with the Confessional Poetry movement, which emphasizes personal and often autobiographical subject matter?

- A. Sylvia Plath
- B. Walt Whitman
- C. Robert Frost
- D. Langston Hughes

## QUESTION 132

"In Shakespeare's play 'Hamlet,' the character of Hamlet himself is one of the most complex and multifaceted in all of literature. Hamlet's internal struggles, his philosophical pondering, and his indecisiveness make him a character who defies easy categorization. Throughout the play, Hamlet grapples with the weight of his father's ghostly command, seeking to avenge his murder. However, his internal turmoil, combined with the political machinations at the Danish court, lead to a tragic and ultimately fatal outcome."

What is a key aspect that contributes to Hamlet's complexity as a character in Shakespeare's play 'Hamlet'?

- A. His unwavering determination to avenge his father's murder.
- B. His ability to easily trust the people around him.
- C. His internal struggles, philosophical pondering, and indecisiveness.
- D. His indifference to the political intrigues at the Danish court.

## QUESTION 133

Which American literary work is considered an example of the Lost Generation literature, reflecting the disillusionment and aimlessness experienced by young people after World War I?

- A. "The Great Gatsby" by F. Scott Fitzgerald
- B. "The Sound and the Fury" by William Faulkner
- C. "The Waste Land" by T.S. Eliot
- D. "Invisible Man" by Ralph Ellison

## QUESTION 134

Which American author is known for her contributions to ecofeminism, a movement that examines the connections between the oppression of women and the destruction of the environment?

- A. Margaret Atwood
- B. Ursula K. Le Guin
- C. Terry Tempest Williams
- D. Louise Erdrich

## QUESTION 135

Which American poet is associated with the Black Arts Movement, a literary and artistic movement that emerged in the 1960s, celebrating Black culture, identity, and political activism?

- A. Maya Angelou
- B. Langston Hughes
- C. Gwendolyn Brooks
- D. Amiri Baraka

## QUESTION 136

What is the term for the biases or prejudices that can be present in visual images in media, affecting how they convey messages?

- A. Filters
- B. Composition
- C. Aesthetics
- D. Stereotypes

QUESTION 137

Which of the following best demonstrates the assessment of the relevance, importance, and sufficiency of evidence in an informational text?

- A. Accepting all provided evidence as equally relevant.
- B. Critically evaluating the quality and relevance of evidence.
- C. Ignoring the evidence and focusing solely on the author's tone.
- D. Summarizing the text without considering the evidence.

QUESTION 138

Which rhetorical appeal relies on appealing to the credibility, authority, and expertise of the speaker to persuade an audience?

- A. Ethos
- B. Pathos
- C. Logos
- D. Kairos

QUESTION 139

How can factors like cultural background, age, and gender influence social norms in interpersonal communication?

- A. They have no influence on social norms.
- B. They can shape expectations and behaviors in communication.
- C. They always lead to conflicts in communication.
- D. They result in universal communication norms.

QUESTION 140

Which region's literature often incorporates elements of magical realism?

- A. Africa
- B. Asia
- C. Latin America
- D. Europe

QUESTION 141

Which rhetorical appeal involves using logical reasoning, evidence, facts, and rational arguments to persuade an audience?

- A. Ethos
- B. Pathos
- C. Logos
- D. Kairos

QUESTION 142

Which of the following is an example of active listening in a conversation?

- A. Checking one's phone for messages while nodding occasionally
- B. Interrupting the speaker to share a personal anecdote
- C. Maintaining eye contact and asking follow-up questions
- D. Avoiding eye contact and remaining silent

## QUESTION 143

The ancient Indian epic "Ramayana" is a significant literary work from which region?

- A. Africa
- B. Asia
- C. Latin America
- D. Europe

## QUESTION 144

In the context of analyzing visual images in media, what is the term for the underlying ideas or concepts conveyed by the images?

- A. Composition
- B. Themes
- C. Filters
- D. Aesthetics

## QUESTION 145

Which technique in collaborative discussions involves evaluating a speaker's point of view, reasoning, and use of evidence by assessing their stance, premises, links between ideas, word choice, points of emphasis, and tone?

- A. Active listening
- B. Critical analysis
- C. Reflective questioning
- D. Mediation

## QUESTION 146

Which rhetorical device involves repeating the same word or phrase at the beginning of successive clauses or sentences for emphasis?

- A. Anaphora
- B. Metonymy
- C. Epistrophe
- D. Synecdoche

## QUESTION 147

Which writing technique involves presenting a series of related ideas or pieces of evidence in a step-by-step or chronological order?

- A. Cause and effect
- B. Comparison and contrast
- C. Sequential order
- D. Spatial order

## QUESTION 148

"In George Orwell's dystopian novel '1984,' the concept of doublethink plays a central role in the Party's manipulation of truth and reality. Doublethink involves the simultaneous acceptance of two contradictory beliefs or ideas, deliberately holding them in one's mind without perceiving the logical inconsistency. This manipulation of language and thought serves as a tool for the totalitarian regime to maintain control over the minds of its citizens. The Party's ability to make citizens believe and accept contradictory statements, such as 'War is Peace' and 'Freedom is Slavery,' exemplifies the extent of their power over thought and language."

How does the concept of doublethink in George Orwell's '1984' serve as a tool for the Party's control over its citizens, and what does it reveal about the power dynamics in the society depicted in the novel?

- A. Doublethink allows citizens to freely express their thoughts and opinions.
- B. Doublethink is a form of collective resistance against the Party's control.
- C. Doublethink enables the Party to manipulate truth and suppress dissent by making citizens accept contradictory beliefs.
- D. Doublethink highlights the citizens' strong belief in the Party's ideology and leadership.

## QUESTION 149

Which writing technique involves using words or phrases that have a specialized meaning within a particular field or domain?

- A. Jargon
- B. Colloquial language
- C. Euphemism
- D. Hyperbole

## QUESTION 150

Which writing technique involves using words or phrases to create connections and transitions between different sections or ideas within a text?

- A. Synonyms
- B. Antonyms
- C. Transitions
- D. Conjunctions

## QUESTION 151

The satirical novel "Gulliver's Travels" was written during which period?

- A. Elizabethan
- B. Victorian
- C. Restoration/Enlightenment
- D. Postcolonial

## QUESTION 152

Which period in British literature is known for its focus on individualism, emotions, and nature?

- A. Romantic
- B. Postcolonial
- C. Anglo-Saxon and Middle Ages
- D. Contemporary

## QUESTION 153

Read the excerpt below from a student's literary analysis essay on the symbolism of the green light in "The Great Gatsby," then answer the question that follows.

"In F. Scott Fitzgerald's novel, the green light serves as a symbol of hope and unattainable dreams. It represents Gatsby's aspirations and his relentless pursuit of his vision of the American Dream. The green light, situated across the water from Gatsby's mansion, becomes a distant beacon of desire that motivates him to strive for wealth and social status."

Which sentence should the student delete during the revision process to eliminate extraneous information?

- A. In F. Scott Fitzgerald's novel, the green light serves as a symbol of hope and unattainable dreams.
- B. It represents Gatsby's aspirations and his relentless pursuit of his vision of the American Dream.
- C. The green light, situated across the water from Gatsby's mansion, becomes a distant beacon of desire.
- D. that motivates him to strive for wealth and social status.

## QUESTION 154

When evaluating the credibility, objectivity, and reliability of sources in an informational text, which action is most appropriate?

- A. Accepting all sources as equally credible.
- B. Disregarding sources that disagree with your personal beliefs.
- C. Assessing the source's reputation, bias, and supporting evidence.
- D. Quoting sources without verifying their accuracy.

## QUESTION 155

Which statement best exemplifies recognizing an accurate summary of an informational text?

- A. A summary that adds personal opinions to enhance the text's meaning.
- B. A summary that captures the main ideas and key details without bias.
- C. A summary that includes irrelevant information from the text.
- D. A summary that uses complex language not found in the original text.

## QUESTION 156

Read the paragraph below from a student's analysis of a Shakespearean sonnet, then answer the question that follows.

"In Sonnet 18, Shakespeare employs vivid imagery to compare his beloved to a summer's day. He highlights the fleeting nature of summer's beauty and contrasts it with the everlasting quality of his beloved's loveliness. By utilizing metaphors and personification, the poet immortalizes his beloved's charm, suggesting that their beauty will be preserved forever in the lines of this sonnet."

Which sentence should the student delete during the revision process to eliminate extraneous information?

- A. In Sonnet 18, Shakespeare employs vivid imagery to compare his beloved to a summer's day.
- B. He highlights the fleeting nature of summer's beauty and contrasts it with the everlasting quality of his beloved's loveliness.
- C. By utilizing metaphors and personification, the poet immortalizes his beloved's charm.
- D. suggesting that their beauty will be preserved forever in the lines of this sonnet.

## QUESTION 157

In assessing the relevance, importance, and sufficiency of evidence in an informational text, what should students be encouraged to do?

- A. Rely solely on the author's authority and expertise.
- B. Ignore evidence that contradicts their prior beliefs.
- C. Consider the quantity and quality of evidence presented.
- D. Accept any evidence presented without questioning.

## QUESTION 158

When evaluating the credibility of sources in a persuasive text, what should students focus on?

- A. The length of the sources.
- B. The author's personal anecdotes.
- C. The source's expertise and evidence.
- D. The font size and formatting.

## QUESTION 159

Which of the following is an example of a rhetorical device commonly used in persuasive texts to enhance their persuasiveness?

- A. Printing the text in a small font size.
- B. Using neutral language throughout.
- C. Employing emotional appeals to evoke feelings.
- D. Avoiding any mention of statistics or facts.

## QUESTION 160

Read the passage below from a student's analysis of a poem exploring the theme of love, then answer the question that follows.

"In the poem, the speaker compares love to a delicate flower that blossoms and wilts with the passage of time. The imagery of vibrant petals opening and withering away symbolizes the transient nature of love's beauty. Through this comparison, the poet suggests that love, like a flower, requires nurturing and care to thrive."

Which sentence should the student delete during the revision process to eliminate extraneous information?

- A. In the poem, the speaker compares love to a delicate flower that blossoms and wilts with the passage of time.
- B. The imagery of vibrant petals opening and withering away symbolizes the transient nature of love's beauty.
- C. Through this comparison, the poet suggests that love, like a flower, requires nurturing and care to thrive.
- D. like a flower, requires nurturing and care to thrive.

## QUESTION 161

Read the excerpt below from a student's analysis of a novel exploring the theme of identity, then answer the question that follows.

"The protagonist's journey of self-discovery is a central theme in the novel. As the narrative unfolds, the character grapples with conflicting societal expectations and personal desires. Through a series of encounters and experiences, the protagonist gradually realizes the importance of embracing their true self and challenging the constraints imposed by society."

Which sentence should the student delete during the revision process to eliminate extraneous information?

- A. The protagonist's journey of self-discovery is a central theme in the novel.
- B. As the narrative unfolds, the character grapples with conflicting societal expectations and personal desires.
- C. Through a series of encounters and experiences, the protagonist gradually realizes the importance of embracing their true self.
- D. and challenging the constraints imposed by society.

## QUESTION 162

Which genre typically focuses on the experiences, challenges, and emotions of young protagonists?

- A. Fiction
- B. Drama
- C. Poetry
- D. Young adult literary texts

## QUESTION 163

Read the following passage from a student's analysis of a short story exploring the theme of isolation, then answer the question that follows.

"The author skillfully depicts the protagonist's profound sense of isolation throughout the narrative. Through vivid descriptions and introspective monologues, readers are immersed in the character's lonely existence. The use of stark imagery and symbolic motifs further enhances the theme of isolation and underscores the character's desperate yearning for connection."

Which sentence should the student delete during the revision process to eliminate extraneous information?

- A. The author skillfully depicts the protagonist's profound sense of isolation throughout the narrative.
- B. Through vivid descriptions and introspective monologues, readers are immersed in the character's lonely existence.
- C. The use of stark imagery and symbolic motifs further enhances the theme of isolation.
- D. and underscores the character's desperate yearning for connection.

## QUESTION 164

Students in a college literature course have analyzed the use of symbolism in a novel. Which of the following activities would enhance their comprehension of the subject?

- A. Identifying and explaining the symbolic significance of key objects or settings in the novel.
- B. Comparing the novel's symbolism to that of another literary work.
- C. Discussing the historical context in which the novel was written.
- D. Summarizing the plot and character development of the novel.

## QUESTION 165

In an advanced English composition class, students have been studying rhetorical devices in persuasive writing. Which of the following activities would enhance their grasp of the subject?

- A. Analyzing a persuasive speech and identifying the rhetorical devices used by the speaker.
- B. Memorizing a list of rhetorical devices and their definitions.
- C. Writing a persuasive essay without incorporating any rhetorical devices.
- D. Reviewing the history and evolution of rhetoric as a discipline.

## QUESTION 166

An Englishclass is exploring the theme of identity in contemporary literature. Which of the following activities would contribute to their comprehension of the theme?

- A. Comparing and contrasting the portrayal of identity in two assigned novels.
- B. Conducting interviews with authors to gain insights into their intentions regarding identity.
- C. Memorizing quotes about identity from literary theorists.
- D. Rewriting a chapter from a novel to present an alternative identity for the protagonist.

## QUESTION 167

The author Isabel Allende is associated with literature from which region?

- A. Africa
- B. Asia
- C. Latin America
- D. Europe

## QUESTION 168

In a poetry course, students have been studying poetic forms and meter. Which of the following activities would enhance their understanding of these concepts?

- A. Analyzing a sonnet and identifying its rhyme scheme and metrical pattern.
- B. Memorizing a glossary of poetic terms and their definitions.
- C. Writing a free verse poem without adhering to any specific meter or rhyme scheme.
- D. Researching the biographies of famous poets to learn about their writing processes.

QUESTION 169

"In Toni Morrison's novel 'Beloved,' the character of Sethe is haunted not only by the ghost of her deceased daughter but also by the traumatic legacy of slavery. Sethe's escape from Sweet Home, a plantation in Kentucky, is a desperate act of liberation from the dehumanizing horrors of slavery. However, the traumatic experiences she endured, including the infanticide she committed to prevent her children from suffering the same fate, continue to haunt her. Sethe's emotional and psychological struggles are emblematic of the broader theme of the enduring trauma of slavery and the quest for individual and collective healing in the aftermath of such a brutal history."

How does Toni Morrison use the character of Sethe in 'Beloved' to explore the theme of the lasting impact of slavery on both individuals and society, and what does Sethe's character symbolize in the context of this exploration?

A. Sethe's character serves as a symbol of uncompromising resistance against oppression, and her experiences represent the strength of the human spirit.
B. Sethe's character represents the complete erasure of individual identity in the face of slavery, highlighting the dehumanizing effects of the institution.
C. Sethe's character illustrates the complexities of survivor guilt and the haunting legacy of slavery, emphasizing the ongoing struggle for healing and redemption.
D. Sethe's character embodies the idealized image of the enslaved as docile and submissive, challenging traditional narratives of resistance during the era of slavery.

QUESTION 170

Read the following passage from a critical analysis of a novel; then answer the question that follows.

"The author employs vivid sensory imagery to immerse readers in the protagonist's world. Through detailed descriptions of sights, sounds, smells, and textures, the author creates a rich and engaging narrative experience. This sensory language not only enhances the reader's understanding of the story but also elicits emotional responses and fosters a deeper connection with the characters."

Which of the following best describes the effect of the author's use of sensory imagery in the novel?

A. It establishes the historical and cultural context of the story.
B. It introduces complex philosophical ideas and themes.
C. It creates a sensory and emotional experience for the reader.
D. It enhances the plot structure and narrative tension.

QUESTION 171

A student is writing an email to a professor to request an extension for a paper. Which of the following sentences would be most appropriate for the student to use as a closing statement?

A. I apologize for any inconvenience caused and appreciate your understanding regarding my situation.
B. I hope this request for an extension is reasonable, and I anticipate a positive response from you.
C. I kindly request that you take my circumstances into consideration and grant me the extension.
D. Please let me know at your earliest convenience if my request for an extension can be accommodated.

QUESTION 172

A student is writing a formal email to a potential internship supervisor to inquire about available opportunities. Which of the following sentences would be most appropriate for the student to use as a closing statement?

A. Thank you for your time and consideration. I look forward to the possibility of working with your organization.
B. If there are any additional documents or information you require, please let me know at your earliest convenience.
C. I hope this email has provided sufficient information, and I eagerly await a positive response from you.
D. I appreciate your attention to my email and expect to hear back from you soon regarding the internship possibilities.

## QUESTION 173

A student is writing an email to a classmate to request notes from a missed lecture. Which of the following sentences would be most appropriate for the student to use as a closing statement?

- A. I understand if you're unable to help, but I would greatly appreciate it if you could provide me with the lecture notes.
- B. Please let me know if you have any questions or concerns, and I hope you're able to assist me with the lecture notes.
- C. I urgently need the lecture notes, so please prioritize my request and send them to me as soon as possible.
- D. Thank you in advance for your assistance. I value your notes, and they will greatly aid in my understanding of the missed lecture.

## QUESTION 174

A student is writing an email to a writing center tutor to request an appointment for assistance with an essay. Which of the following sentences would be most appropriate for the student to use as a closing statement?

- A. I believe your expertise would greatly benefit my writing, so I eagerly await confirmation of my appointment.
- B. I hope my request for an appointment is not burdensome, and I would be grateful for your assistance.
- C. Please consider my request for an appointment, as I believe your guidance will enhance my essay significantly.
- D. Thank you for considering my appointment request. I look forward to meeting you and discussing my essay in detail.

## QUESTION 175

In a persuasive editorial arguing for stricter environmental regulations, what is the author's likely purpose?

- A. To entertain readers with humorous anecdotes
- B. To inform readers about the history of environmental policies
- C. To persuade readers to support stricter environmental regulations
- D. To critique the flaws in existing environmental legislation

## QUESTION 176

Which of the following is an effective organizational approach often used in narrative writing?

- A. Listing random thoughts and ideas as they come to mind
- B. Jumping back and forth between different time periods without a clear order
- C. Presenting events in the order they occurred, from beginning to end
- D. Starting the narrative with the conclusion and working backward

## QUESTION 177

"In F. Scott Fitzgerald's novel 'The Great Gatsby,' the character of Jay Gatsby is a mysterious and enigmatic figure whose persona is built upon layers of illusion and self-invention. Gatsby's extravagant parties, his opulent mansion, and his reputation as a wealthy and successful man all contribute to the mystique surrounding him. However, as the narrative unfolds, it becomes clear that Gatsby's wealth is a facade created to win the love of Daisy Buchanan, his unrequited love from the past. The dichotomy between Gatsby's public persona and his private aspirations serves as a commentary on the American Dream and the superficiality of wealth and social status."

How does F. Scott Fitzgerald use the character of Jay Gatsby in 'The Great Gatsby' to critique the concept of the American Dream and the pursuit of wealth and social status, and what does Gatsby's character reveal about the disillusionment that can accompany this pursuit?

- A. Gatsby's character exemplifies the attainability of the American Dream through hard work and determination, emphasizing the aspirational nature of the novel.
- B. Gatsby's character embodies the idea that wealth and social status are the ultimate markers of success, reflecting the prevailing values of the Jazz Age.
- C. Gatsby's character symbolizes the hollowness of the American Dream when pursued solely for material gain, highlighting the eventual disillusionment and emptiness it can bring.
- D. Gatsby's character represents the unrelenting pursuit of wealth as the path to happiness, challenging traditional notions of success in American literature.

QUESTION 178

A writer develops the topic sentence below for a paragraph in an expository essay about William Shakespeare.

"William Shakespeare, widely regarded as the greatest playwright in English literature, has left an indelible mark on the world of drama."

Which of the following supporting details would be most effective for the writer to use in the paragraph with this topic sentence?

- A. Shakespeare's plays encompass various genres such as tragedy, comedy, and historical fiction, demonstrating his versatility as a playwright.
- B. Born in Stratford-upon-Avon, Shakespeare lived during the Elizabethan era, a time of great cultural and artistic flourishing in England.
- C. Shakespeare's works have been translated into multiple languages and continue to be performed and studied worldwide, showcasing their enduring popularity.
- D. Many of Shakespeare's plays explore timeless themes such as love, power, and ambition, resonating with audiences across different time periods and cultures.

QUESTION 179

A writer develops the topic sentence below for a paragraph in an expository essay about the effects of climate change.

"The consequences of climate change are far-reaching and pose significant challenges to the environment and human societies."

Which of the following supporting details would be most effective for the writer to use in the paragraph with this topic sentence?

- A. Rising global temperatures contribute to the melting of polar ice caps, leading to rising sea levels and endangering coastal regions.
- B. Climate change is a controversial topic, with some individuals denying its existence or downplaying its potential impact.
- C. The Earth's climate has experienced natural variations throughout history, but the current rate and extent of climate change are largely attributed to human activities.
- D. Efforts to mitigate climate change include transitioning to renewable energy sources, reducing greenhouse gas emissions, and promoting sustainable practices.

QUESTION 180

A writer develops the topic sentence below for a paragraph in an expository essay about the impact of social media on society.

"Social media platforms have revolutionized communication and transformed various aspects of modern life."

Which of the following supporting details would be most effective for the writer to use in the paragraph with this topic sentence?

- A. Social media has given rise to cyberbullying, with individuals experiencing harassment, threats, and the spread of harmful content online.
- B. Many people spend excessive amounts of time on social media, which can lead to reduced productivity, social isolation, and negative mental health effects.
- C. Social media platforms provide opportunities for businesses and individuals to reach a global audience, enhance brand awareness, and facilitate networking.
- D. Privacy concerns related to social media usage have become a significant issue, with personal data being collected and potentially misused by various entities.

QUESTION 181

In a persuasive text, what should students look for when assessing the objectivity of the content?

- A. A clear presentation of both sides of the argument.
- B. A strong bias in favor of the author's viewpoint.
- C. A focus on logical reasoning and evidence.
- D. The use of persuasive language techniques.

QUESTION 182

Which aspect of graphic features, such as photographs and illustrations, in persuasive texts should students interpret?

- A. The artistic quality of the images.
- B. How the images make them feel.
- C. The potential bias or manipulation in the images.
- D. The physical dimensions of the images.

QUESTION 183

What is a common purpose of using repetition in a persuasive text?

- A. To confuse the reader.
- B. To make the text longer.
- C. To emphasize key points and ideas.
- D. To avoid presenting evidence.

QUESTION 184

In a persuasive text, what is the primary purpose of employing the Toulmin model of argumentation?

- A. To create complex sentence structures.
- B. To outline the structure of the author's argument.
- C. To appeal exclusively to the reader's emotions.
- D. To include humor and satire.

QUESTION 185

A participant in a panel discussion makes the introductory statement below.

"In literature, the theme of love has been explored extensively, often portraying its complexities, joys, and sorrows."

Which of the following responses to this introductory statement would most effectively build on the participant's ideas and move the discussion forward?

- A. Many renowned authors, such as Shakespeare and Jane Austen, have delved into the theme of love, presenting different perspectives and illustrating the various facets of this powerful emotion.
- B. The portrayal of love in literature reflects societal norms and expectations, highlighting the influence of cultural and historical contexts on the understanding of romantic relationships.
- C. Love as a theme in literature can be interpreted through various genres, including poetry, novels, and plays, allowing for diverse representations and explorations of this universal human experience.
- D. It is intriguing how love is not limited to romantic relationships in literature but can also manifest in familial bonds, friendships, and even the love for one's country, expanding the scope and significance of this theme.

QUESTION 186

What is the primary purpose of integrating a summary effectively into a text while maintaining the flow of ideas?

- A. To avoid referencing sources in academic writing.
- B. To confuse readers by presenting different viewpoints.
- C. To condense the source material and support your argument.
- D. To highlight the credibility of the original source.

QUESTION 187

When is it most appropriate to use a direct quotation in academic writing?

- A. When you want to save space in your paper.
- B. When you want to express your own viewpoint.
- C. When the original wording is essential for your argument.
- D. When you want to avoid citing sources.

QUESTION 188

A participant in a panel discussion makes the introductory statement below.

"The influence of technology on education has been transformative, revolutionizing the way students learn and interact with information."

Which of the following responses to this introductory statement would most effectively build on the participant's ideas and move the discussion forward?

- A. The integration of technology in education has enabled personalized learning experiences, catering to individual students' needs and promoting self-directed learning.
- B. The excessive use of technology in classrooms may lead to students' decreased attention spans, diminished critical thinking abilities, and overreliance on digital resources.
- C. Traditional teaching methods are becoming obsolete in the face of advancing technology, urging educators to adapt their instructional practices and embrace innovative approaches that leverage digital tools.
- D. With the proliferation of online learning platforms, educational opportunities have become more accessible to marginalized communities, bridging the gap in education and empowering individuals to pursue knowledge.

QUESTION 189

A participant in a panel discussion makes the introductory statement below.

"Art has the power to evoke emotions, challenge societal norms, and provoke thought."

Which of the following responses to this introductory statement would most effectively build on the participant's ideas and move the discussion forward?

- A. Artistic expression can provide a platform for marginalized voices, giving them agency and allowing for the exploration of social justice issues.
- B. Artists often push boundaries and question established norms, leading to controversy and debates surrounding the freedom of artistic expression.
- C. The evolution of technology has opened new avenues for artistic creation and engagement, blurring the boundaries between traditional art forms and digital media.
- D. Art appreciation is subjective, with individuals interpreting and connecting with artworks based on their unique perspectives, experiences, and cultural backgrounds.

## QUESTION 190

A participant in a panel discussion makes the introductory statement below.

"The use of symbolism in literature enhances readers' understanding by imbuing objects, characters, or actions with deeper meaning."

Which of the following responses to this introductory statement would most effectively build on the participant's ideas and move the discussion forward?

- A. Symbolism can create a sense of universality in literature, allowing readers from different backgrounds to connect with the underlying themes and messages conveyed through symbolic elements.
- B. The interpretation of symbols in literature is subjective and can vary depending on readers' personal experiences, cultural contexts, and literary analysis frameworks.
- C. Authors employ symbolism to add layers of complexity to their works, inviting readers to engage in deeper analysis and uncover hidden layers of meaning.
- D. The use of symbolism in literature can transcend language barriers, enabling the translation and appreciation of symbolic elements across different cultures and societies.

## QUESTION 191

When analyzing the use of ethos, pathos, and logos in a persuasive text, which of the following represents "logos"?

- A. Appeals to emotions and feelings.
- B. Appeals to the credibility and authority of the speaker.
- C. Appeals to logic and reasoning.
- D. Appeals to the cultural values of the audience.

## QUESTION 192

In the context of persuasive writing, what is the primary purpose of employing the Rogerian argument strategy?

- A. To use humor and satire to persuade.
- B. To avoid addressing counterarguments.
- C. To find common ground with opposing viewpoints.
- D. To create an emotionally charged atmosphere.

## QUESTION 193

Which of the following best demonstrates the appropriate use of paraphrasing in an academic text?

- A. Copying a sentence verbatim from the source without citation.
- B. Rewriting a source's ideas using identical words and sentence structure.
- C. Expressing a source's ideas in your own words and citing the source.
- D. Using the source's wording and giving credit only at the end of the paragraph.

QUESTION 194

Read the passage below; then answer the question that follows.

In his groundbreaking research, Dr. Johnson has uncovered a direct correlation between sleep deprivation and impaired cognitive function. Through rigorous experimentation and analysis of data, he has demonstrated that individuals who consistently lack sufficient sleep exhibit reduced mental acuity and diminished problem-solving abilities. These findings have significant implications for understanding the importance of sleep in maintaining optimal cognitive performance.

Which of the following sentences best conveys the main idea of the passage while being clear and concise?

A. Dr. Johnson's research reveals a strong link between sleep deprivation and impaired cognitive function, emphasizing the crucial role of sleep for optimal mental performance.
B. Through extensive experimentation and data analysis, Dr. Johnson has conclusively proven that inadequate sleep leads to reduced mental acuity and impaired problem-solving abilities, highlighting the significance of sleep for cognitive performance.
C. Dr. Johnson's groundbreaking research indicates a clear correlation between sleep deprivation and diminished cognitive function, underscoring the vital role of sleep in maintaining optimal mental capabilities.
D. Extensive research by Dr. Johnson demonstrates a direct association between sleep deprivation and impaired cognitive function, emphasizing the necessity of sleep for optimal cognitive performance.

QUESTION 195

Read the paragraph below; then answer the question that follows.

The documentary, a compelling and thought-provoking exploration of climate change, offers a comprehensive analysis of its causes, consequences, and potential solutions. By presenting scientific evidence, expert interviews, and real-life examples, the film effectively engages viewers and raises awareness about the urgent need for environmental action. Furthermore, it motivates individuals to adopt sustainable practices and become active participants in mitigating the effects of climate change.

Which of the following statements best summarizes the paragraph while maintaining clarity and conciseness?

A. The documentary explores climate change, analyzing its causes, consequences, and solutions, and motivates viewers to take action.
B. Through scientific evidence, expert interviews, and real-life examples, the documentary effectively raises awareness about climate change, encouraging viewers to adopt sustainable practices and take part in mitigating its effects.
C. The documentary presents a comprehensive analysis of climate change, engaging viewers with compelling content that emphasizes the need for environmental action and individual involvement.
D. By examining climate change and its causes, consequences, and solutions, the documentary motivates viewers to become active participants in addressing the issue and adopting sustainable practices.

QUESTION 196

A group of college English students is analyzing a complex poem. Which of the following activities would enhance their understanding of the poem?

A. Identifying and discussing the use of literary devices in the poem.
B. Memorizing and reciting the poem to improve comprehension.
C. Comparing the poem to a completely unrelated work of literature.
D. Creating a visual representation of the poem's overall structure.

QUESTION 197

An Englishclass has just finished reading a novel and wants to explore the author's writing style further. Which of the following activities would be most beneficial for this purpose?

A. Analyzing the novel's characters and their development throughout the story.
B. Writing a short essay on personal reflections and reactions to the novel.
C. Researching the author's biography and discussing its influence on their writing.
D. Comparing the novel to a popular movie adaptation and discussing the differences.

## QUESTION 198

An Englishcourse is studying different forms of poetry. Which of the following activities would be most effective in helping students analyze the poetic elements of a specific poem?

- A. Collaboratively rewriting the poem in modern language.
- B. Identifying the rhyme scheme and meter of the poem.
- C. Creating a physical representation of the poem using art supplies.
- D. Presenting a dramatic performance of the poem to the class.

## QUESTION 199

In an Englishliterature course, students are studying a play by a contemporary playwright. Which of the following activities would best deepen their understanding of the play?

- A. Participating in a roundtable discussion to analyze the play's themes and symbols.
- B. Rewriting the ending of the play to explore alternative resolutions.
- C. Conducting a survey among classmates to determine their favorite character.
- D. Creating a collage of images representing key moments in the play.

## QUESTION 200

Read the passage below from Virginia Woolf's novel To the Lighthouse (1927); then answer the question that follows.

Yes, she thought, laying down her brush in extreme fatigue, I have had my vision.

Which of the following best describes the tone of the passage?

- A. Contentment
- B. Desolation
- C. Weariness
- D. Exhilaration

## QUESTION 201

Read the excerpt below from Langston Hughes's poem "Harlem" (1951); then answer the question that follows.

What happens to a dream deferred?

Does it dry up

like a raisin in the sun?

Or fester like a sore—

And then run?

Which of the following literary devices is most prominently used in this excerpt?

- A. Simile
- B. Metaphor
- C. Hyperbole
- D. Allusion

QUESTION 202

What is the primary purpose of persuasive writing?

- A. To provide a neutral analysis of a topic.
- B. To entertain readers with fictional stories.
- C. To educate readers about a historical event.
- D. To state an opinion or influence beliefs.

QUESTION 203

When it comes to establishing a clear position or controlling idea in persuasive writing, what is a crucial step?

- A. Avoiding any mention of counterarguments.
- B. Presenting multiple contradictory positions.
- C. Clearly stating the central argument or viewpoint.
- D. Providing a lengthy and detailed background.

QUESTION 204

A student is writing an argumentative essay advocating for the inclusion of LGBTQ+ literature in high school English curricula. Which of the following sentences should the student present first in the essay?

- A. Introducing LGBTQ+ literature in high school classrooms promotes inclusivity and diversity, providing students with a broader understanding of society.
- B. Engaging with LGBTQ+ literature can help students develop empathy and compassion towards individuals from diverse backgrounds.
- C. Research shows that exposure to LGBTQ+ literature positively impacts students' mental health and overall well-being.
- D. Incorporating LGBTQ+ literature into the curriculum prepares students to navigate an increasingly diverse world and promotes acceptance.

QUESTION 205

An Englishteacher is designing a lesson on effective thesis statements for persuasive essays. Which of the following sentences should the teacher present first in the lesson?

- A. A strong thesis statement clearly articulates the main argument and provides a roadmap for the essay.
- B. Writing a persuasive essay requires a well-developed thesis statement that engages the reader from the start.
- C. A thesis statement is the backbone of a persuasive essay, guiding the writer's arguments and serving as a focal point for the reader.
- D. Crafting a compelling thesis statement involves carefully analyzing the topic and formulating a clear stance.

QUESTION 206

An English teacher is discussing the role of foreshadowing in literature. Which of the following sentences should the professor present first in the lecture?

- A. Foreshadowing serves as a literary device that hints at future events, creating suspense and engaging the reader.
- B. Skillful use of foreshadowing allows authors to deepen the meaning of their work and enhance the reader's experience.
- C. Readers who pay attention to foreshadowing can make predictions about the plot, contributing to their enjoyment and involvement with the text.
- D. By strategically incorporating foreshadowing, authors can surprise readers with unexpected plot twists and revelations.

QUESTION 207

An English teacher is teaching a lesson on effective transitions in writing. Which of the following sentences should the instructor present first in the lesson?

- A. Transitions serve as bridges between ideas, helping readers navigate smoothly through the text.
- B. Effective use of transitions improves the flow and coherence of writing, enhancing the reader's understanding.
- C. Well-placed transitions enable writers to present their arguments logically and cohesively.
- D. Using transitional phrases and words strengthens the connections between sentences and paragraphs.

QUESTION 208

An English teacher is assigning a group project that involves analyzing a complex literary text. The professor decides to provide a detailed rubric outlining the expectations for each section of the project. This approach will contribute to the project's success in which of the following ways?

- A. Guiding students in understanding the specific requirements and objectives of each project component.
- B. Ensuring that each student has an equal workload and responsibility within the group.
- C. Encouraging students to think critically and independently during the analysis process.
- D. Facilitating effective collaboration and coordination among group members.

QUESTION 209

An English teacher assigns a research paper to the class and emphasizes the importance of using credible and authoritative sources. This approach will contribute to the students' research skills in which of the following ways?

- A. Enabling students to develop an informed and balanced perspective on the research topic.
- B. Enhancing students' ability to evaluate and critically analyze different sources of information.
- C. Fostering students' creativity and originality in presenting their research findings.
- D. Encouraging students to rely on personal anecdotes and experiences to support their arguments.

QUESTION 210

An English teacher introduces the concept of close reading to students and provides them with a short story to analyze. This approach will contribute to the students' literary analysis skills in which of the following ways?

- A. Encouraging students to explore the cultural and historical context of the short story.
- B. Developing students' ability to identify and analyze literary devices employed by the author.
- C. Fostering students' creativity in generating alternative interpretations of the short story.
- D. Promoting students' collaboration and discussion skills through group analysis of the short story.

QUESTION 211

What is a common method of selecting an effective organizational approach in persuasive writing?

- A. Using random ideas and examples.
- B. Presenting information in chronological order.
- C. Organizing points based on their length.
- D. Structuring the text logically or by importance.

QUESTION 212

Which of the following strategies is most effective for introducing a topic and developing it thoroughly in an informational or explanatory text?

- A. Including personal anecdotes and experiences to engage the reader.
- B. Providing a concise summary of the topic without elaboration.
- C. Selecting and presenting the most significant and relevant facts, examples, or information.
- D. Using abstract concepts and theoretical frameworks to present the topic.

QUESTION 213

Which rhetorical appeal aims to evoke emotions and create an emotional connection with the audience?

- A. Ethos
- B. Pathos
- C. Logos
- D. Kairos

## QUESTION 214

In persuasive writing, why is it important to acknowledge and address counterarguments?

- A. To confuse the reader with conflicting information.
- B. To prove that counterarguments are always wrong.
- C. To strengthen your own argument by showing its superiority.
- D. To ignore opposing viewpoints for the sake of simplicity.

## QUESTION 215

Which of the following is an example of an effective organizational approach in persuasive writing?

- A. Mixing unrelated ideas in no particular order.
- B. Presenting the strongest point first and the weakest last.
- C. Repeating the same argument throughout the text.
- D. Structuring the text with a clear introduction, body, and conclusion.

## QUESTION 216

An English teacher assigns a group presentation where students have to analyze a famous speech from history. The professor encourages students to incorporate multimedia elements, such as visuals and audio clips, to enhance their presentation. This approach will contribute to the students' presentation skills in which of the following ways?

- A. Engaging the audience and enhancing their understanding of the speech's historical context.
- B. Ensuring equal participation and contribution from all group members during the presentation.
- C. Promoting effective time management and organization of the presentation materials.
- D. Encouraging students to focus on delivering persuasive arguments and rhetorical techniques.

# Chapter 2 – Answers and Explanations

**QUESTION 1**

**Answer:** B

**Explanation:** Drama is characterized by its emphasis on dialogue and stage directions, as it is meant to be performed on stage or screen.

**QUESTION 2**

**Answer:** B

**Explanation:** The connotative meaning of a word goes beyond its literal definition and includes emotional or cultural associations. In this case, "home" is associated with feelings of warmth, comfort, and belonging, making option B the correct choice.

**QUESTION 3**

**Answer:** D

**Explanation:** Dialects are regional variations of language that influence pronunciation, vocabulary, and sometimes syntax. These variations are shaped by regional factors, making option D the correct choice.

**QUESTION 4**

**Answer:** D

**Explanation:** The main idea is the central theme or purpose of the text. In this case, the main idea is to emphasize the importance of addressing climate change for the benefit of future generations, making option D the correct choice.

**QUESTION 5**

**Answer:** C

**Explanation:** The phrase "War is Peace, Freedom is Slavery, Ignorance is Strength" contains contradictory terms, making it an oxymoron. This literary device is used in '1984' to emphasize the oppressive and manipulative nature of the government's propaganda. It presents seemingly contradictory ideas to illustrate the twisted logic of the totalitarian regime, where contradictory statements are presented as facts to control and manipulate the citizens.

**QUESTION 6**

**Answer:** C

**Explanation:** Poetry is known for its use of language, including rhyme, rhythm, and poetic devices, to create a specific emotional or intellectual impact.

**QUESTION 7**

**Answer:** D

**Explanation:** The myth of the Minotaur is a story from Greek mythology and is thus associated with European literature. It is set in the labyrinth of King Minos of Crete and involves the hero Theseus.

**QUESTION 8**

**Answer:** C

**Explanation:** Hyperbole involves intentional exaggeration to make a point or evoke strong emotions, often for comedic effect.

## QUESTION 9

**Answer:** C

**Explanation:** "Amorous" is a derivative of the Latin word "amare," which means "to love." It relates to romantic or passionate love, making it the correct choice.

## QUESTION 10

**Answer:** A

**Explanation:** The Renaissance, a period of cultural and intellectual growth in Europe, had a profound impact on English vocabulary through the borrowing of words from Latin and Greek, making option A the correct choice.

## QUESTION 11

**Answer:** A

**Explanation:** "Malevolent" is an antonym of "benevolent," as it means having or showing a desire to harm others, whereas "benevolent" means well-meaning and kind.

## QUESTION 12

**Answer:** A

**Explanation:** Theme represents the underlying concept or ideas explored in a literary work, providing insight into its deeper meaning.

## QUESTION 13

**Answer:** D

**Explanation:** Analyzing similar themes or topics involves examining how different texts explore and present common themes or subjects.

## QUESTION 14

**Answer:** C

**Explanation:** Authors often draw inspiration from prior literary texts and traditions but transform them to develop their own unique and original works.

## QUESTION 15

**Answer:** B

**Explanation:** The intended audience for a text on advanced astrophysics theories is likely to be individuals with a background in the field, such as college professors and researchers, making option B the correct choice.

## QUESTION 16

**Answer:** B

**Explanation:** Specific details provide precise information about a particular topic. Option B provides specific information about why Mars is called the "Red Planet," making it the correct choice.

## QUESTION 17

**Answer:** D

**Explanation:** Text coherence examines how individual sentences, paragraphs, and larger portions of the text relate to one another, creating a cohesive whole.

## QUESTION 18

**Answer:** D

**Explanation:** Interpreting words and phrases involves understanding the non-literal or symbolic meanings of language used by the author.

## QUESTION 19

**Answer:** D

**Explanation:** Word choice analysis involves evaluating the deliberate selection of words by the author and how they contribute to the overall meaning, tone, and mood of the text.

## QUESTION 20

**Answer:** A

**Explanation:** Fiction encompasses imaginative storytelling through the creation of characters, settings, and plot, typically using prose.

## QUESTION 21

**Answer:** B

**Explanation:** Drama relies on acts, scenes, and theatrical conventions to present its narrative on stage or screen.

## QUESTION 22

**Answer:** C

**Explanation:** Meter in poetry involves the rhythmic pattern of stressed and unstressed syllables, which contributes to the overall flow and musicality of the poem.

## QUESTION 23

**Answer:** C

**Explanation:** Analyzing text structure involves assessing how specific sentences, paragraphs, or sections of a text relate to one another and contribute to the overall meaning and structure.

## QUESTION 24

**Answer:** D

**Explanation:** The line "To be or not to be, that is the question" contains a stark contrast between the concepts of existence and non-existence, which is a characteristic of antithesis. This literary device is used to emphasize Hamlet's internal conflict and the fundamental question he is grappling with regarding life and death.

## QUESTION 25

**Answer:** D

**Explanation:** Analyzing the impact of specific word choices helps to reveal how the author's deliberate language selections contribute to the text's overall meaning, tone, and mood.

## QUESTION 26

**Answer:** B

**Explanation:** The correct response provides a clear and accurate definition of theme, emphasizing that it goes beyond the genre or literary devices used, and focuses on the underlying message or central idea of a text.

QUESTION 27

Answer: A

Explanation: The most effective approach would involve a comparative analysis of the settings and characters in the two texts, as it would provide concrete evidence of how social inequality is depicted and explored in each work.

QUESTION 28

Answer: D

Explanation: A persuasive speech on gun control laws is generally intended for the general public and policymakers to advocate for a specific change in policy, making option D the correct choice.

QUESTION 29

Answer: C

Explanation: The author's point of view in a persuasive article arguing for increased funding for public schools is typically in favor of the proposed action, which is to increase funding for public education, making option C the correct choice.

QUESTION 30

Answer: C

Explanation: The professor should focus on how the author draws upon and transforms prior literary texts and traditions by analyzing how themes, characters, or storylines from previous works are incorporated and modified in the author's own original work.

QUESTION 31

Answer: C

Explanation: To understand the impact of specific word choices on the poem's meaning, tone, and mood, the student should focus on the figurative language, such as metaphors or similes, used by the author to create vivid imagery and evoke certain emotions or atmospheres.

QUESTION 32

Answer: D

Explanation: The most effective approach would involve analyzing the transitions and connections between sentences and paragraphs to understand how they contribute to the overall structure and coherence of the novel.

QUESTION 33

Answer: A

Explanation: "Beowulf" is an epic poem that originated in the Anglo-Saxon and Middle Ages period, specifically in the 8th to 11th centuries.

QUESTION 34

Answer: C

Explanation: The central idea of a persuasive advertisement is to highlight the benefits or advantages of the product or service being promoted, which, in this case, is the new electric car model, making option C the correct choice.

QUESTION 35

Answer: C

Explanation: Propaganda often employs emotional appeals and presents information in a one-sided manner to influence and persuade the audience, making option C the correct choice.

## QUESTION 36

**Answer:** A

**Explanation:** William Shakespeare's works, such as "Romeo and Juliet" and "Hamlet," are typically associated with the Elizabethan period, which coincided with Queen Elizabeth I's reign.

## QUESTION 37

**Answer:** C

**Explanation:** Technical texts like warranties and contracts typically use specialized language and legal terminology to ensure clarity and specificity in their content, making option C the correct choice.

## QUESTION 38

**Answer:** C

**Explanation:** The primary purpose of a warranty document is to provide clear information about the terms and conditions of the product's coverage, including any warranties or guarantees, making option C the correct choice.

## QUESTION 39

**Answer:** A

**Explanation:** "Jane Eyre" was written during the Victorian period, which spanned from the mid-19th to early 20th century, and it explores themes of love, social class, and feminism.

## QUESTION 40

**Answer:** A

**Explanation:** "Waiting for Godot" is a play written in the mid-20th century and is considered a significant work of the Modern period, known for its experimentation and existential themes.

## QUESTION 41

**Answer:** A

**Explanation:** The Postcolonial period in British literature emerged as a response to the dismantling of the British Empire and explores themes of colonialism, identity, and cultural clashes.

## QUESTION 42

**Answer:** C

**Explanation:** "Pride and Prejudice" was written during the Restoration/Enlightenment period and reflects the social and moral values of that time, particularly regarding courtship and marriage.

## QUESTION 43

**Answer:** A

**Explanation:** The Restoration/Enlightenment period emphasized reason, logic, and scientific advancements, with thinkers like John Locke and Isaac Newton shaping the intellectual landscape.

## QUESTION 44

**Answer:** A

**Explanation:** "Frankenstein" was written during the Romantic period and explores themes of nature, ambition, and the consequences of scientific advancement.

## QUESTION 45

**Answer:** A

**Explanation:** High school English teachers should instruct students to identify logical fallacies, including ad hominem attacks, which involve attacking the person instead of addressing the argument directly.

## QUESTION 46

**Answer:** C

**Explanation:** A "call to action" is a persuasive technique that urges the audience to act in a certain way. High school English teachers should teach students to recognize and understand this technique, making option C the correct choice.

## QUESTION 47

**Answer:** A

**Explanation:** The Victorian period was characterized by social realism, industrialization, and a strong focus on class divisions, as seen in works like Charles Dickens' novels.

## QUESTION 48

**Answer:** A

**Explanation:** T.S. Eliot was a prominent poet of the Modern period, known for his innovative style and exploration of existential themes in works like "The Waste Land."

## QUESTION 49

**Answer:** B

**Explanation:** The "in medias res" approach involves starting a narrative in the midst of action or at a critical moment, which can engage readers immediately and create intrigue, making option B the correct choice.

## QUESTION 50

**Answer:** B

**Explanation:** High school English teachers should emphasize the importance of proper citation to give credit to original authors and avoid plagiarism, as demonstrated in option B.

## QUESTION 51

**Answer:** C

**Explanation:** High school English teachers should teach students to use in-text citations within the text and provide a bibliography or reference list to acknowledge sources appropriately, as described in option C.

## QUESTION 52

**Answer:** C

**Explanation:** The English Renaissance period saw the decline of feudalism and the rise of the middle class, accompanied by cultural and artistic flourishing, including the works of William Shakespeare.

## QUESTION 53

**Answer:** A

**Explanation:** "An Inspector Calls" was written in the mid-20th century and addresses social issues, class divisions, and moral responsibility, aligning it with the concerns of the Modern period.

## QUESTION 54

**Answer:** A

**Explanation:** The Contemporary period in British literature, spanning from the mid-20th century to the present, is known for its postmodern features, including metafiction and intertextuality.

## QUESTION 55

**Answer:** D

**Explanation:** The Generative theory, proposed by Noam Chomsky, suggests that humans are born with an innate ability to acquire language and possess a universal grammar that guides language development.

## QUESTION 56

**Answer:** C

**Explanation:** Inferring is the reading strategy that involves drawing logical conclusions and making educated guesses about the text based on prior knowledge and textual evidence.

## QUESTION 57

**Answer:** A

**Explanation:** Phonological processing refers to the ability to process and manipulate sounds in spoken language. Difficulties in this area can lead to challenges in accurately and fluently recognizing words, a common characteristic of language-based reading disabilities.

## QUESTION 58

**Answer:** C

**Explanation:** Communicative language teaching emphasizes using the target language for real-life communication and meaningful interactions. It focuses on developing learners' fluency and accuracy through authentic language use.

## QUESTION 59

**Answer:** D

**Explanation:** Monitoring is a comprehension strategy that involves actively checking and evaluating one's understanding of the text while reading. It helps readers identify and address any comprehension gaps or confusion that may arise.

## QUESTION 60

**Answer:** B

**Explanation:** Including a counterargument helps establish the significance of a claim by acknowledging and addressing opposing viewpoints, demonstrating an understanding of the complexity of the issue being argued.

## QUESTION 61

**Answer:** D

**Explanation:** The body paragraphs of an argumentative essay provide the logical structure for organizing claims, counterclaims, reasons, and evidence, presenting a coherent and well-structured argument.

QUESTION 62

Answer: C

Explanation: In the context of the excerpt, 'To the Lighthouse' is described as a modernist novel that employs stream-of-consciousness narrative techniques to explore the inner thoughts of characters. Modernism is indeed a literary movement characterized by experimentation with narrative techniques and an emphasis on the interior lives of characters, which aligns with the description provided.

QUESTION 63

Answer: C

Explanation: The main purpose of an informational text on healthy eating habits is typically to provide readers with knowledge and guidance on making nutritious food choices, making option C the correct choice.

QUESTION 64

Answer: C

Explanation: Transition words, such as "however," "therefore," and "in addition," help link the major sections of a text, create cohesion, and clarify the relationships between claim(s), reasons, evidence, and counterclaims.

QUESTION 65

Answer: C

Explanation: To develop claims and counterclaims fairly and thoroughly, it is important to supply the most relevant evidence for each, acknowledging the strengths and limitations of both in a manner that anticipates the audience's knowledge level, concerns, values, and biases.

QUESTION 66

Answer: D

Explanation: A concluding statement or section in an argumentative essay should tie together the main points and evidence presented in the essay, providing a final statement that supports and follows from the argument made throughout the essay.

QUESTION 67

Answer: C

Explanation: General statements provide broad information about a topic. Option C discusses the transformative impact of the internet on society in general, making it the correct choice.

QUESTION 68

Answer: D

Explanation: Reflection is a narrative technique that allows the author to delve into a character's inner world, providing insights into their thoughts, emotions, and motivations.

QUESTION 69

Answer: D

Explanation: Orientation in narrative writing involves setting out a problem, situation, or observation, along with its significance, to engage the reader from the beginning.

## QUESTION 70

**Answer:** C

**Explanation:** Functional texts like timetables and application forms are designed to present information in a clear and organized manner, making it easy for readers to find and understand the information they need, making option C the correct choice.

## QUESTION 71

**Answer:** C

**Explanation:** Consumer contracts provide consumers with information about their rights and responsibilities regarding a product or service, making option C the correct choice.

## QUESTION 72

**Answer:** D

**Explanation:** Multimedia refers to the integration of various media forms, including digital media and visual displays, to enhance communication. By using visual aids, presenters can make complex information more accessible, engage the audience, and strengthen their persuasive message.

## QUESTION 73

**Answer:** C

**Explanation:** Chronological order is a technique used to sequence events in the order they occur, creating a coherent narrative where events build on one another logically and chronologically.

## QUESTION 74

**Answer:** B

**Explanation:** Subplots are additional storylines within a narrative that run parallel to the main plot, adding complexity, depth, and alternative perspectives to the overall story.

## QUESTION 75

**Answer:** A

**Explanation:** Figurative language, such as metaphors, similes, and sensory descriptions, enhances the narrative by using vivid and imaginative language to paint a vivid picture in the reader's mind.

## QUESTION 76

**Answer:** C

**Explanation:** Exposition is a technique that combines informative and explanatory writing within a narrative, providing necessary background information, context, or explanations to enhance the reader's understanding.

## QUESTION 77

**Answer:** C

**Explanation:** The denouement is the concluding part of a narrative that follows the climax and provides a sense of resolution. It reflects on what has been experienced, observed, or resolved over the course of the narrative.

## QUESTION 78

**Answer:** A

**Explanation:** Dialogue is a narrative technique that involves characters' direct speech, providing insights into their thoughts, emotions, interactions, and advancing the plot.

## QUESTION 79

**Answer:** C

**Explanation:** The primary purpose of a timetable for public transportation is to provide clear and accurate information about departure and arrival times for the convenience of passengers, making option C the correct choice.

## QUESTION 80

**Answer:** B

**Explanation:** Foreshadowing is a technique used to hint at or suggest future events, outcomes, or developments in a narrative, creating a sense of anticipation and building toward a particular tone or outcome.

## QUESTION 81

**Answer:** A

**Explanation:** "Things Fall Apart" is a novel by Chinua Achebe, a renowned Nigerian author. It explores the impact of colonialism on Igbo society in Nigeria and is considered a significant work in African literature.

## QUESTION 82

**Answer:** A

**Explanation:** Haiku is a traditional form of Japanese poetry consisting of three lines and a syllable structure of 5-7-5. It is closely associated with Asian literature, particularly Japanese literature.

## QUESTION 83

**Answer:** C

**Explanation:** "One Hundred Years of Solitude" is a novel by Gabriel Garcia Marquez, a Colombian author. It is considered a masterpiece of Latin American literature and explores the Buendía family's experiences in the fictional town of Macondo.

## QUESTION 84

**Answer:** B

**Explanation:** "Wide Sargasso Sea" is a novel by Jean Rhys, a Dominican-born British author. It serves as a prequel to Charlotte Brontë's "Jane Eyre" and explores the story of Bertha Mason, the "madwoman in the attic."

## QUESTION 85

**Answer:** D

**Explanation:** "Hamlet" is a tragedy written by William Shakespeare, an English playwright. It is one of Shakespeare's most famous works and is widely regarded as a masterpiece of European literature.

## QUESTION 86

**Answer:** A

**Explanation:** "The Bhagavad Gita" is a sacred Hindu scripture and an integral part of the ancient Indian epic, the Mahabharata. It is considered a significant text in Asian literature, particularly in the context of Hindu philosophy.

## QUESTION 87

**Answer:** C

**Explanation:** Effective narrative writing often involves selecting a specific aspect or moment that is most relevant to the intended message or theme, rather than trying to include every possible detail, making option C the correct choice.

## QUESTION 88

**Answer:** C

**Explanation:** Including an anecdote about an unexpected adventure adds interest and excitement to the narrative, making it more engaging for readers and relevant to the topic, making option C the correct choice.

## QUESTION 89

**Answer:** C

**Explanation:** The primary purpose of narrative writing is to entertain and engage the reader by sharing a story or personal experience, making option C the correct choice.

## QUESTION 90

**Answer:** A

**Explanation:** In the excerpt, Gatsby's mansion, parties, and pursuit of wealth are described as symbols of his aspiration to attain the American Dream. This use of objects to represent deeper meanings aligns with the literary device of symbolism, as indicated in option A. These symbols convey the idea that Gatsby's wealth and extravagance are a reflection of his pursuit of the American Dream.

## QUESTION 91

**Answer:** B

**Explanation:** Pablo Neruda was a Chilean poet and diplomat who won the Nobel Prize in Literature. His works, such as "Twenty Love Poems and a Song of Despair," made significant contributions to Latin American literature.

## QUESTION 92

**Answer:** D

**Explanation:** "Madame Bovary" is a novel written by Gustave Flaubert, a French author. It is considered a classic of European literature and portrays the life and struggles of Emma Bovary.

## QUESTION 93

**Answer:** A

**Explanation:** Derek Walcott, a Caribbean poet and playwright, is known for his epic poem "Omeros." This work explores themes of identity, colonialism, and Caribbean history, making it a significant contribution to the region's literature.

## QUESTION 94

**Answer:** C

**Explanation:** "Dracula" is a novel by Bram Stoker, an Irish author. It is a classic example of the Gothic genre, known for its atmospheric setting, supernatural elements, and themes of horror and suspense.

## QUESTION 95

**Answer:** C

**Explanation:** Technology, particularly the internet and digital communication, has greatly influenced the development of Standard American English. It has allowed for the rapid dissemination of language, leading to the emergence of new vocabulary, abbreviations, and expressions. Social media platforms, texting, and online forums have also contributed to the evolution of language and the formation of new linguistic conventions within Standard American English. Therefore, Option C is the correct answer as it acknowledges the positive influence of technology on the development and expansion of Standard American English.

## QUESTION 96

**Answer:** A

**Explanation:** When encountering an unfamiliar word, relying on contextual clues within the sentence or passage is often the most effective strategy for determining its meaning. The surrounding words, phrases, and sentence structure can provide valuable hints about the word's intended definition. While consulting a thesaurus or conducting an etymological analysis can provide additional insights, they may not always be readily available or practical. Identifying and analyzing the word's morphological components can be helpful in some cases, particularly with prefixes, suffixes, or root words, but it is not always a reliable strategy. Therefore, Option A is the correct answer as it emphasizes the importance of using semantic and syntactic clues in understanding word meanings.

## QUESTION 97

**Answer:** B

**Explanation:** General academic vocabulary refers to words and phrases that are commonly used across various academic disciplines and subject areas. It includes terms and concepts that are relevant to a broad range of academic contexts. On the other hand, domain-specific vocabulary is limited to a particular field, discipline, or profession. It consists of terms and jargon that are specific to that particular domain and may not be commonly understood outside of it. Therefore, Option B accurately describes the distinction between general academic and domain-specific vocabulary, making it the correct answer.

## QUESTION 98

**Answer:** C

**Explanation:** Engaging in extensive reading is a highly effective technique for vocabulary acquisition through context and word study. By reading extensively, individuals encounter words in various contexts, allowing for a deeper understanding of their meanings, nuances, and usage. This approach also enables learners to grasp the relationships between words and their surrounding context, facilitating a more holistic understanding of vocabulary. While memorizing lists of isolated vocabulary words and utilizing flashcards can be useful for some learners, they often lack meaningful context and may not promote long-term retention and application. Focusing solely on the analysis of word roots and affixes can enhance word recognition skills but may not provide a comprehensive understanding of vocabulary in meaningful contexts. Therefore, Option C is the correct answer as it emphasizes the importance of extensive reading for vocabulary acquisition.

## QUESTION 99

**Answer:** C

**Explanation:** One common barrier to effective listening is having preconceived judgments or biases about the speaker or the topic, which can hinder open and unbiased listening, making option C the correct choice.

## QUESTION 100

**Answer:** C

**Explanation:** Restating or paraphrasing what someone has said is a method of active participation that shows you are actively listening and trying to ensure you understand the speaker's perspective, making option C the correct choice.

## QUESTION 101

**Answer:** A

**Explanation:** The denotative meaning of a word refers to its literal or dictionary definition, whereas the connotative meaning of a word encompasses the emotions, associations, or cultural implications it carries beyond its literal definition. In the given example, the denotative meaning of "home" is a place where someone lives, which is the basic dictionary definition. However, the connotative meaning of "home" goes beyond the physical space and evokes a sense of warmth, comfort, and belonging. It is the emotional and subjective response associated with the word. Option a) accurately represents the distinction between denotative and connotative meanings by providing an example that highlights both aspects of the word "home," making it the correct answer.

## QUESTION 102

**Answer:** D

**Explanation:** Refutation is a rhetorical strategy that involves acknowledging and addressing counterarguments or opposing viewpoints in order to strengthen one's own argument. By refuting opposing claims, a writer demonstrates their ability to consider alternative perspectives and provides evidence or reasoning to support their position. This strategy enhances the writer's credibility (ethos) by showing their willingness to engage with differing opinions and strengthens the logical appeal (logos) of their argument. Therefore, Option D is the correct answer as it accurately identifies the rhetorical strategy of refutation.

## QUESTION 103

**Answer:** C

**Explanation:** Cultural factors play a significant role in both spoken and written communication. Culture influences the ways in which language is used, including the choice of words, idiomatic expressions, tone, and gestures. It also affects how messages are interpreted and understood by different individuals or communities. Cultural norms, values, beliefs, and social contexts all contribute to variations in language use and communication styles. Therefore, Option C accurately reflects the role of cultural factors in shaping spoken and written communication, making it the correct answer.

## QUESTION 104

**Answer:** C

**Explanation:** Adapting the tone, style, and language to suit the specific audience, purpose, and context is the most effective strategy for writing effectively in various situations. Writing is a communicative act, and tailoring the message to the intended audience ensures that it is understood and engages the readers appropriately. This may involve using different levels of formality, adjusting vocabulary and sentence structure, and considering the cultural, social, or professional expectations of the audience. Options a) and b) emphasize specific approaches that may not be suitable for all audiences or purposes, while Option D limits the effectiveness of the writing by relying solely on personal opinions. Therefore, Option C is the correct answer as it emphasizes the importance of adapting the writing style to achieve effective communication.

## QUESTION 105

**Answer:** C

**Explanation:** The stage of revising involves reviewing and improving the overall organization, coherence, and effectiveness of a written text. During this stage, writers focus on the structure and flow of their ideas, ensuring that the content is logically organized, coherent, and well-developed. They may make substantial changes to the content, rearrange paragraphs, clarify arguments, or strengthen the overall impact of the text. While planning involves generating ideas and outlining the structure, drafting involves producing a rough version of the text, and editing focuses on correcting grammar and language errors, it is during the revising stage that the writer critically evaluates and enhances the content and structure of the text. Therefore, Option C is the correct answer.

## QUESTION 106

**Answer:** C

**Explanation:** Engaging in peer editing or seeking feedback from knowledgeable individuals is the most effective strategy for editing written texts to achieve conformity with conventions of Standard English usage. Peer editors or knowledgeable individuals can provide valuable insights and suggestions regarding grammar, sentence structure, word choice, and overall language proficiency. They can identify errors or inconsistencies that may have been overlooked by the writer. Relying solely on grammar and spell-checking software may not catch all errors, especially those related to contextual usage or style. Consulting a thesaurus for synonyms can be helpful for improving vocabulary variety but does not guarantee conformity with language conventions. Ignoring minor errors undermines the importance of accuracy and adherence to standard language conventions. Therefore, Option C is the correct answer as it promotes the effective editing of written texts.

## QUESTION 107

**Answer:** C

**Explanation:** When developing a conclusion for an informational or explanatory text, it is most appropriate to summarize the main points and provide a final thought or insight. This approach reinforces the main content of the text and allows the reader to review and reflect on the information presented. Introducing new ideas or topics unrelated to the main content can confuse the reader and detract from the coherence of the text. Restating the introduction verbatim may not provide new information or contribute to the overall understanding of the topic. Ending abruptly without a concluding statement leaves the text incomplete and fails to provide a satisfying closure. Therefore, Option C is the correct answer as it emphasizes the importance of summarizing the main points and offering a final thought or insight.

## QUESTION 108

**Answer:** C

**Explanation:** An effective way to use precise language and domain-specific vocabulary when informing or explaining a topic is to balance their use with explanations or definitions for clarity. While domain-specific vocabulary is appropriate and necessary in certain contexts, it is important to consider the readers' understanding and provide appropriate context or explanations to ensure comprehension. Overloading the text with technical jargon can alienate readers who are not familiar with the specific terminology. Avoiding specific terms and using general language may oversimplify the topic and fail to convey the necessary precision and depth of understanding. Using figurative language and metaphors may be more suitable for literary or creative texts rather than informational or explanatory texts. Therefore, Option C is the correct answer as it emphasizes the importance of balancing domain-specific vocabulary with explanations or definitions.

## QUESTION 109

**Answer:** C

**Explanation:** Appropriate and varied transitions in an informational or explanatory text serve the key function of linking the major sections of the text and creating cohesion. Transitions help guide the reader through the text by signaling shifts in ideas, providing continuity, and establishing logical connections between different parts of the text. Confusing the reader and creating ambiguity undermines the clarity and effectiveness of the text. While providing a chronological account may be suitable in certain cases, it does not encompass the broader range of transitions that contribute to cohesion. Introducing unrelated ideas and concepts disrupts the flow and coherence of the text. Therefore, Option C is the correct answer as it highlights the importance of transitions in linking major sections and creating cohesion.

## QUESTION 110

**Answer:** C

**Explanation:** Employing irony to create a humorous tone is an example of using a literary device to affect meaning in an informational or explanatory text. Irony involves conveying a meaning that is the opposite of what is expected or a situation that is contrary to what is anticipated. By using irony, the writer can engage the reader, add depth to the text, and create a humorous effect. While using vivid sensory details can enhance the reader's understanding and engagement, it does not specifically involve a literary device. Incorporating dialogue between characters may be more common in narrative or fictional texts rather than informational or explanatory texts. Using figurative language to convey emotions can add impact, but it may not directly affect the meaning in an informational or explanatory context. Therefore, Option C is the correct answer as it exemplifies the use of irony to affect meaning in an informational or explanatory text.

## QUESTION 111

**Answer:** B

**Explanation:** Conducting preliminary research before developing a focused research question is the most effective technique for developing a research question and narrowing or broadening inquiry as appropriate. This approach allows the researcher to explore the existing literature, identify gaps in knowledge, and gain a better understanding of the topic. It helps refine the research question by considering the available information and potential avenues for inquiry. Stating a general topic without specific research objectives lacks the necessary focus and direction for meaningful research. Limiting inquiry to a single perspective or point of view limits the breadth and depth of the research. Adopting a fixed research question without flexibility for adjustments may hinder the researcher's ability to adapt and refine the inquiry based on emerging findings. Therefore, Option B is the correct answer as it emphasizes the importance of conducting preliminary research to develop a focused research question.

## QUESTION 112

**Answer:** C

**Explanation:** When assessing the strengths and limitations of prospective sources in terms of task, purpose, audience, and credibility, it is most appropriate to evaluate the currency, relevance, and reliability of the source. Currency refers to the timeliness of the information, relevance refers to its applicability to the research topic or question, and reliability refers to the trustworthiness and accuracy of the source. Relying solely on popular sources may not guarantee credibility or relevance to the research. Considering the author's personal background and experiences can provide some insights but should not be the sole criterion for assessing credibility. Assessing the visual appeal and design of the source material is important for aesthetic purposes but does not directly relate to the source's reliability or relevance. Therefore, Option C is the correct answer as it emphasizes the evaluation of currency, relevance, and reliability in assessing prospective sources.

## QUESTION 113

**Answer:** C

**Explanation:** Quoting directly from multiple sources and providing proper citations is the most effective technique for integrating information into a text selectively while avoiding plagiarism and overreliance on any one source. Quoting allows the writer to directly include relevant and authoritative information while providing credit to the original source. It ensures transparency and credibility while maintaining the development of ideas. Copying and pasting large portions of text from a single source can lead to plagiarism and overreliance on a single perspective. Paraphrasing extensively without proper citation may still result in unintentional plagiarism if the original ideas are not properly credited. Excluding all external sources limits the depth and breadth of the research and may result in an incomplete or biased perspective. Therefore, Option C is the correct answer as it highlights the importance of quoting directly from multiple sources and providing proper citations.

## QUESTION 114

**Answer:** D

**Explanation:** Adhering to a specific citation style guide recommended by the academic or publishing institution is the most important technique for citing material accurately using a standard format. Different fields and disciplines often have specific style guides (such as APA, MLA, Chicago, etc.) that provide guidelines for citing sources in a consistent and standardized manner. Following a specific citation style guide ensures clarity, consistency, and proper attribution of sources. Including citations only for direct quotations disregards the importance of acknowledging and citing paraphrased information. Using any citation format may introduce inconsistencies and confusion. Consulting a variety of citation style guides may result in inconsistency and lack of adherence to a specific standard. Therefore, Option D is the correct answer as it emphasizes the importance of adhering to a specific citation style guide recommended by the academic or publishing institution.

## QUESTION 115

**Answer:** C

**Explanation:** Nonverbal cues, such as facial expressions, gestures, and body language, are primarily used to convey emotions, feelings, and intentions during a conversation, making option C the correct choice.

## QUESTION 116

**Answer:** C

**Explanation:** Adapting the structure and style to suit the specific requirements and expectations is the most effective technique for presenting information by using appropriate structure and style for the task, purpose, and audience. This approach ensures that the presentation is tailored to the specific context and effectively communicates the intended message. Utilizing complex and technical language may alienate the audience and hinder comprehension. Using a casual and conversational tone may not be suitable for all contexts and can compromise the professionalism of the presentation. Including personal anecdotes and unrelated tangents may distract from the main content and dilute the focus of the presentation. Therefore, Option C is the correct answer as it emphasizes the importance of adapting the structure and style to suit the specific requirements and expectations.

## QUESTION 117

**Answer:** B

**Explanation:** Transcendentalism was a philosophical and literary movement that celebrated individualism, spiritual unity with nature, and the inherent goodness of humans. Prominent Transcendentalist writers include Ralph Waldo Emerson and Henry David Thoreau.

## QUESTION 118

**Answer:** C

**Explanation:** Zora Neale Hurston's novel "Their Eyes Were Watching God" is a prominent work of the Harlem Renaissance, showcasing African American culture, folk traditions, and the search for self-identity.

## QUESTION 119

**Answer:** C

**Explanation:** Modernism emerged in the early 20th century and reflected the changing social, political, and technological landscape. Modernist writers, such as T.S. Eliot and Virginia Woolf, often employed fragmented narratives and explored themes of alienation and the human condition.

## QUESTION 120

**Answer:** A

**Explanation:** Jack Kerouac, known for his novel "On the Road," is a prominent figure of the Beat Generation. The Beat writers rejected mainstream culture and sought liberation and enlightenment through alternative lifestyles.

## QUESTION 121

**Answer:** D

**Explanation:** E.E. Cummings was an innovative poet who experimented with language and visual arrangement on the page. His unique style often played with lowercase letters, punctuation, and unconventional word order.

## QUESTION 122

**Answer:** C

**Explanation:** Satire is a genre that uses irony, humor, and exaggeration to criticize or ridicule human vices, follies, and institutions. Works like Jonathan Swift's "Gulliver's Travels" and Mark Twain's "The Adventures of Huckleberry Finn" are notable examples of satire.

## QUESTION 123

**Answer:** C

**Explanation:** "House of Leaves" is a postmodern novel known for its unconventional formatting, multiple narrators, and intricate plot. It pushes the boundaries of storytelling and engages readers in a complex exploration of perception and reality.

## QUESTION 124

**Answer:** C

**Explanation:** Composition involves the arrangement of visual elements within the frame of an image, influencing how viewers perceive and interpret the image, making option C the correct choice.

## QUESTION 125

**Answer:** C

**Explanation:** Image manipulation is the process of altering visual images in media to achieve specific goals, such as influencing public opinion or changing personal behavior, making option C the correct choice.

## QUESTION 126

Answer: C

Explanation: Personal experience and prior knowledge can influence how individuals perceive and interpret visual images, as their background and context affect their understanding and meaning-making, making option C the correct choice.

## QUESTION 127

Answer: D

Explanation: Toni Morrison is renowned for her powerful novels, such as "Beloved" and "The Bluest Eye," which tackle issues of race, identity, and the traumatic legacy of slavery. Her works shed light on the experiences of African Americans in America.

## QUESTION 128

Answer: D

Explanation: Ethnic literature refers to the literary works produced by writers from specific ethnic or cultural backgrounds, addressing their experiences, struggles, and cultural heritage. It often explores themes of identity, immigration, and discrimination.

## QUESTION 129

Answer: C

Explanation: Samuel Beckett, an Irish playwright, is known for his plays such as "Waiting for Godot" that exemplify the Theater of the Absurd. His works often feature absurd situations, repetitive dialogue, and explore the meaninglessness of human existence.

## QUESTION 130

Answer: B

Explanation: Mark Twain's novel "The Adventures of Tom Sawyer" is a prime example of regionalism, as it vividly portrays life along the Mississippi River and explores the distinct culture and dialect of the American Midwest.

## QUESTION 131

Answer: A

Explanation: Sylvia Plath is known for her intensely personal and emotionally raw poetry, addressing themes of mental illness, gender, and identity. Her confessional style of writing had a significant impact on the development of Confessional Poetry.

## QUESTION 132

Answer: C

Explanation: Hamlet's complexity primarily arises from his internal struggles, philosophical contemplation, and indecisiveness throughout the play. These traits make him a multifaceted character who grapples with complex moral and emotional dilemmas, contributing to the depth of his character in 'Hamlet.'

## QUESTION 133

Answer: A

Explanation: F. Scott Fitzgerald's novel "The Great Gatsby" captures the spirit of the Lost Generation, exploring themes of wealth, social status, and the hollowness of the American Dream in the post-war era.

## QUESTION 134

**Answer:** C

**Explanation:** Terry Tempest Williams is an American writer and environmental activist whose works, such as "Refuge: An Unnatural History of Family and Place," combine personal narratives with environmental awareness, advocating for the protection of the natural world.

## QUESTION 135

**Answer:** D

**Explanation:** Amiri Baraka, formerly known as LeRoi Jones, was a prominent figure in the Black Arts Movement. His poetry and plays, such as "Dutchman" and "SOS: Poems 1961-2013," address racial inequality, Black consciousness, and the struggle for civil rights.

## QUESTION 136

**Answer:** D

**Explanation:** Stereotypes refer to biases or prejudices present in visual images that can influence how they convey messages, often by relying on simplified or exaggerated portrayals of certain groups or ideas, making option D the correct choice.

## QUESTION 137

**Answer:** B

**Explanation:** High school English teachers should teach students to critically assess the quality and relevance of evidence in informational texts. Option B reflects this approach, as it emphasizes the importance of evaluating evidence rather than blindly accepting it.

## QUESTION 138

**Answer:** A

**Explanation:** Ethos is an appeal to the credibility and trustworthiness of the speaker. By establishing their expertise, qualifications, and trustworthiness, the speaker aims to gain the audience's confidence and persuade them based on their authority.

## QUESTION 139

**Answer:** B

**Explanation:** Cultural background, age, and gender can influence social norms and expectations in interpersonal communication, leading to variations in communication styles and behaviors, making option B the correct choice.

## QUESTION 140

**Answer:** C

**Explanation:** Magical realism is a literary style that blends fantastical elements with reality. It is commonly associated with Latin American literature, exemplified by works like "One Hundred Years of Solitude" by Gabriel Garcia Marquez

## QUESTION 141

**Answer:** C

**Explanation:** Logos is an appeal to logic and reason. It involves presenting well-structured arguments, providing evidence, using statistics, and making logical connections to convince the audience through reasoned discourse.

## QUESTION 142

**Answer:** C

**Explanation:** Active listening involves maintaining engagement with the speaker by making eye contact and asking follow-up questions to show interest and understanding, making option C the correct choice.

## QUESTION 143

**Answer:** B

**Explanation:** "Ramayana" is an ancient Indian epic that holds great cultural and religious importance in Asian literature. It narrates the story of Prince Rama and his adventures in rescuing his wife Sita from the demon king Ravana.

## QUESTION 144

**Answer:** B

**Explanation:** Themes represent the underlying ideas or concepts conveyed by visual images in media, providing a deeper understanding of the message, making option B the correct choice.

## QUESTION 145

**Answer:** B

**Explanation:** Critical analysis involves carefully evaluating a speaker's arguments, evidence, and rhetorical strategies. It requires assessing the speaker's position, the soundness of their reasoning, the effectiveness of their evidence, and the persuasive techniques employed to make informed judgments about the presentation.

## QUESTION 146

**Answer:** A

**Explanation:** Anaphora is the deliberate repetition of a word or phrase at the beginning

## QUESTION 147

**Answer:** C

**Explanation:** Sequential order, also known as chronological order or step-by-step order, is a writing technique that presents information or ideas in a logical sequence. It is commonly used when explaining a process or narrating events in the order they occur.

## QUESTION 148

**Answer:** C

**Explanation:** In '1984,' doublethink is a tool used by the Party to control its citizens by making them accept contradictory beliefs without questioning, which serves to manipulate truth and suppress dissent. It reveals the totalitarian regime's power to shape reality and control the minds of its citizens through linguistic manipulation and psychological conditioning.

## QUESTION 149

**Answer:** A

**Explanation:** Jargon is specialized vocabulary used within a specific field or domain. It helps to communicate precise meanings to those familiar with the subject matter but may be unfamiliar or confusing to those outside of that field.

## QUESTION 150

**Answer:** C

**Explanation:** Transitions are words, phrases, or sentences that establish logical connections between ideas, clarify relationships, and create cohesion within a text. They help readers navigate the flow of information and understand how different concepts relate to one another.

## QUESTION 151

**Answer:** C

**Explanation:** "Gulliver's Travels" was written by Jonathan Swift and is a satirical work that reflects the social and political ideas of the Restoration/Enlightenment period.

## QUESTION 152

**Answer:** A

**Explanation:** The Romantic period emphasized individualism, intense emotions, and a connection to nature, with notable poets such as William Wordsworth and Samuel Taylor Coleridge.

## QUESTION 153

**Answer:** D

**Explanation:** "that motivates him to strive for wealth and social status." This sentence repeats the information already conveyed in the previous sentence and does not provide any new insights. Removing it would improve the paragraph's conciseness without sacrificing important details.

## QUESTION 154

**Answer:** C

**Explanation:** High school English teachers should encourage students to critically evaluate sources based on their reputation, potential bias, and the evidence they provide. Option C reflects this practice.

## QUESTION 155

**Answer:** B

**Explanation:** High school English teachers should teach students to create unbiased and accurate summaries of informational texts. Option B reflects this approach by emphasizing the importance of capturing the main ideas and key details without introducing bias or personal opinions.

## QUESTION 156

**Answer:** D

**Explanation:** "suggesting that their beauty will be preserved forever in the lines of this sonnet." This sentence restates the idea already expressed in the previous sentence and does not provide any additional insights. Removing it would streamline the paragraph and eliminate redundant information.

## QUESTION 157

**Answer:** C

**Explanation:** High school English teachers should guide students to consider both the quantity and quality of evidence when assessing its relevance and sufficiency. Option C reflects this practice by emphasizing these crucial factors in evidence evaluation.

## QUESTION 158

**Answer:** C

**Explanation:** High school English teachers should guide students to assess the credibility of sources in persuasive texts based on the source's expertise and the quality of evidence presented. Option C reflects this practice.

## QUESTION 159

**Answer:** C

**Explanation:** High school English teachers should teach students to recognize rhetorical devices like emotional appeals in persuasive texts. Option C reflects the use of such a device to engage readers emotionally.

## QUESTION 160

**Answer:** D

**Explanation:** "like a flower, requires nurturing and care to thrive." This sentence repeats the idea already expressed in the previous sentence and does not provide any new insights. Removing it would streamline the passage and eliminate redundant information.

## QUESTION 161

**Answer:** D

**Explanation:** "and challenging the constraints imposed by society." This sentence restates the idea already expressed in the previous sentence and does not provide any additional insights. Removing it would streamline the passage and eliminate redundant information.

## QUESTION 162

**Answer:** D

**Explanation:** Young adult literary texts specifically target adolescent readers and often explore themes relevant to their lives.

## QUESTION 163

**Answer:** D

**Explanation:** "and underscores the character's desperate yearning for connection." This sentence restates the idea already expressed in the previous sentence and does not provide any additional insights. Removing it would streamline the passage and eliminate redundant information.

## QUESTION 164

**Answer:** A

**Explanation:** Option A would deepen students' understanding of symbolism by requiring them to identify and explain the symbolic significance of specific elements within the novel. This activity allows students to engage with the text on a deeper level and analyze the author's use of symbolism to convey themes or messages.

## QUESTION 165

**Answer:** A

**Explanation:** Option A would deepen students' understanding of rhetorical devices by requiring them to analyze a persuasive speech and identify the specific devices used by the speaker. This activity encourages students to apply their knowledge and develop their skills in recognizing and interpreting rhetorical techniques in real-world examples.

## QUESTION 166

**Answer:** A

**Explanation:** Option A would deepen students' understanding of the theme of identity by requiring them to compare and contrast how different novels portray this concept. This activity encourages critical thinking, analysis, and the ability to identify commonalities and differences in the treatment of identity across different literary works.

## QUESTION 167

**Answer:** C

**Explanation:** Isabel Allende is a Chilean author known for her works such as "The House of the Spirits." She is recognized as a prominent figure in Latin American literature, blending historical events and magical realism in her writing.

QUESTION 168

Answer: A

Explanation: Option A would deepen students' understanding of poetic forms and meter by requiring them to analyze a specific poem, such as a sonnet, and identify its rhyme scheme and metrical pattern. This activity allows students to apply their knowledge in a practical manner and develop their skills in recognizing and analyzing different poetic structures.

QUESTION 169

Answer: C

Explanation: Sethe's character in 'Beloved' represents the complex emotional and psychological effects of slavery, including survivor guilt and the lasting trauma of the institution. She symbolizes the broader theme of the enduring impact of slavery on both individuals and society, emphasizing the ongoing quest for healing and redemption in the face of such a brutal history.

QUESTION 170

Answer: C

Explanation: The author's use of sensory imagery in the novel creates a sensory and emotional experience for the reader. By vividly describing sights, sounds, smells, and textures, the author allows readers to engage their senses and form a more immersive connection with the story and its characters. This technique brings the narrative to life and evokes emotional responses in the reader.

QUESTION 171

Answer: A

Explanation: This option acknowledges any inconvenience caused by the student's request and expresses appreciation for the professor's understanding. It maintains a polite and respectful tone, which is appropriate for addressing a professor.

QUESTION 172

Answer: A

Explanation: This option conveys gratitude for the recipient's time and consideration, while expressing genuine interest in the possibility of working with their organization. It concludes the email on a positive note, leaving a favorable impression.

QUESTION 173

Answer: D

Explanation: The correct answer is D. This option expresses gratitude in advance for the assistance, acknowledges the value of the classmate's notes, and highlights the benefits it would provide the student in understanding the missed lecture. It maintains a polite tone and is more likely to elicit a positive response.

QUESTION 174

Answer: D

Explanation: This option expresses appreciation for considering the appointment request and conveys enthusiasm for the upcoming meeting. It creates a positive expectation and sets a friendly tone for the interaction with the writing center tutor.

QUESTION 175

Answer: C

Explanation: The purpose of a persuasive editorial is typically to convince the audience of a specific viewpoint or action, in this case, supporting stricter environmental regulations, making option C the correct choice.

## QUESTION 176

**Answer:** C

**Explanation:** Chronological order is a common and effective organizational approach in narrative writing, as it helps readers follow the sequence of events in a clear and logical manner, making option C the correct choice.

## QUESTION 177

**Answer:** C

**Explanation:** Jay Gatsby's character serves as a critique of the pursuit of wealth and social status for their own sake, highlighting the emptiness and disillusionment that can result from such a single-minded pursuit of the American Dream. Fitzgerald uses Gatsby's story to comment on the superficiality of material success and the inherent hollowness of the dream when it is divorced from deeper values and meaning.

## QUESTION 178

**Answer:** C

**Explanation:** This supporting detail emphasizes the global impact of Shakespeare's works, highlighting their translation, performance, and ongoing study worldwide. It aligns with the topic sentence by emphasizing the lasting influence of Shakespeare in the world of drama.

## QUESTION 179

**Answer:** A

**Explanation:** This supporting detail highlights one of the consequences of climate change—rising sea levels due to the melting of polar ice caps. It directly connects to the topic sentence by illustrating the far-reaching effects of climate change on the environment and human societies.

## QUESTION 180

**Answer:** C

**Explanation:** This supporting detail highlights the transformative aspect of social media by emphasizing its impact on businesses, brand awareness, and networking opportunities. It aligns with the topic sentence's assertion that social media has revolutionized communication and transformed aspects of modern life.

## QUESTION 181

**Answer:** A

**Explanation:** High school English teachers should encourage students to assess the objectivity of persuasive texts by looking for a balanced presentation of different viewpoints. Option A reflects this practice.

## QUESTION 182

**Answer:** C

**Explanation:** High school English teachers should guide students to interpret graphic features in persuasive texts by considering the potential bias or manipulation in the images used to support the argument. Option C reflects this analytical approach.

## QUESTION 183

**Answer:** C

**Explanation:** High school English teachers should teach students that repetition in persuasive texts is often used to emphasize and reinforce key points or ideas. Option C reflects this purpose of repetition in persuasive writing.

## QUESTION 184

**Answer:** B

**Explanation:** The Toulmin model is a sophisticated tool for analyzing and constructing arguments. High school English teachers should teach students how to use it to outline the structure of persuasive texts, making option B the correct choice.

## QUESTION 185

**Answer:** C

**Explanation:** This response effectively builds on the participant's idea by highlighting the diverse genres in which the theme of love is explored in literature. It acknowledges the multi-faceted nature of love and the flexibility of its representation across different literary forms.

## QUESTION 186

**Answer:** C

**Explanation:** High school English teachers should teach students how to integrate summaries effectively to condense source material and provide support for their arguments, as depicted in option C.

## QUESTION 187

**Answer:** C

**Explanation:** High school English teachers should guide students to use direct quotations when the original wording is crucial to their argument, as indicated in option C.

## QUESTION 188

**Answer:** A

**Explanation:** This response effectively builds on the participant's idea by emphasizing the transformative impact of technology on education, specifically highlighting the benefits of personalized learning experiences and self-directed learning. It expands on the notion of technology revolutionizing learning and provides a positive perspective on its influence.

## QUESTION 189

**Answer:** B

**Explanation:** This response effectively builds on the participant's idea by focusing on the challenging aspect of art and its ability to question societal norms. It acknowledges the potential for controversy and the debates surrounding freedom of artistic expression, expanding the discussion beyond emotions and thought-provocation.

## QUESTION 190

**Answer:** C

**Explanation:** This response effectively builds on the participant's idea by emphasizing the role of symbolism in adding complexity to literary works and encouraging deeper analysis. It expands the discussion by highlighting the reader's engagement with symbolism and the potential for uncovering hidden layers of meaning.

## QUESTION 191

**Answer:** C

**Explanation:** Ethos, pathos, and logos are rhetorical appeals. High school English teachers should instruct students that "logos" refers to appeals based on logic and reasoning, making option C the correct choice.

## QUESTION 192

**Answer:** C

**Explanation:** The Rogerian argument strategy aims to build consensus by finding common ground with opposing viewpoints. High school English teachers should teach students this advanced technique for handling arguments, making option C the correct choice.

## QUESTION 193

**Answer:** C

**Explanation:** High school English teachers should instruct students on the proper use of paraphrasing, which involves restating ideas in their own words while providing proper citation, as shown in option C.

## QUESTION 194

**Answer:** A

**Explanation:** Option A concisely conveys the main idea of the passage by emphasizing the link between sleep deprivation and impaired cognitive function, as well as the importance of sleep for optimal mental performance. It captures the key findings and highlights the significance of the research while maintaining clarity and conciseness.

## QUESTION 195

**Answer:** B

**Explanation:** Option B succinctly summarizes the paragraph by highlighting the documentary's exploration of climate change, its use of scientific evidence, expert interviews, and real-life examples to raise awareness, and its emphasis on encouraging viewers to adopt sustainable practices and take part in mitigating the effects of climate change. The statement maintains clarity and conciseness while capturing the main points of the paragraph.

## QUESTION 196

**Answer:** A

**Explanation:** Option A is the most appropriate choice as it involves analyzing and discussing the use of literary devices in the poem. This activity helps students gain a deeper understanding of the poem's meaning, symbolism, and artistic techniques, which are crucial for interpreting complex poems.

## QUESTION 197

**Answer:** C

**Explanation:** Option C is the most suitable choice as it involves researching the author's biography and discussing its influence on their writing style. By understanding the author's background and experiences, students can gain insights into the motivations behind the author's writing choices and enhance their understanding of the novel's unique style.

## QUESTION 198

**Answer:** B

**Explanation:** Option B is the most appropriate choice as it involves identifying the rhyme scheme and meter of the poem. This activity allows students to focus on the structural and rhythmic elements of the poem, which are fundamental to understanding and analyzing poetry. It helps students appreciate the poet's use of sound and rhythm to convey meaning.

## QUESTION 199

**Answer:** A

**Explanation:** Option A is the most suitable choice as it involves participating in a roundtable discussion to analyze the play's themes and symbols. This activity encourages critical thinking and engages students in a thoughtful examination of the play's deeper meaning. It allows them to explore different perspectives and interpretations, enriching their understanding of the play as a whole.

## QUESTION 200

Answer: C

Explanation: The correct answer is C, weariness. The passage conveys a sense of exhaustion and fatigue as indicated by phrases such as "laying down her brush in extreme fatigue" and the emphasis on having had a vision, suggesting that the narrator's energy has been expended. The tone reflects a state of weariness rather than contentment, desolation, or exhilaration.

## QUESTION 201

Answer: A

Explanation: The correct answer is A, simile. A simile is a figure of speech that compares two unlike things using "like" or "as." In this excerpt, the lines "Does it dry up like a raisin in the sun?" and "Or fester like a sore—" both present comparisons using "like." The similes are used to create vivid imagery and convey the potential consequences of a deferred dream.

## QUESTION 202

Answer: D

Explanation: The primary purpose of persuasive writing is to express a viewpoint and persuade the reader to adopt that perspective, as indicated in option D.

## QUESTION 203

Answer: C

Explanation: In persuasive writing, it's essential to clearly articulate the central argument or position to guide the reader, as emphasized in option C.

## QUESTION 204

Answer: A

Explanation: Option A should be presented first in the essay because it introduces the main argument by emphasizing the benefits of including LGBTQ+ literature in high school English curricula. It sets the tone for the essay and establishes the central theme of promoting inclusivity and diversity. The other options provide supporting points or evidence, but they rely on the initial premise presented in Option A.

## QUESTION 205

Answer: A

Explanation: Option A should be presented first in the lesson as it provides a concise and comprehensive definition of a strong thesis statement. It sets the foundation for understanding the purpose and importance of an effective thesis statement in persuasive essays. The other options offer additional insights into thesis statements, but they build upon the introductory concept presented in Option A.

## QUESTION 206

Answer: A

Explanation: Option A should be presented first in the lecture as it provides a clear definition and explanation of foreshadowing. It introduces the purpose and impact of foreshadowing on the reader's experience. The other options expand upon the significance and effects of foreshadowing, but they rely on the initial concept established in Option A.

## QUESTION 207

Answer: A

Explanation: Option A should be presented first in the lesson as it provides a concise definition of transitions and their purpose. It establishes the foundational concept that transitions act as bridges between ideas, guiding the reader's comprehension and facilitating smooth transitions between sentences and paragraphs. The other options elaborate on the importance and benefits of transitions, but they build upon the introductory idea presented in Option A.

## QUESTION 208

**Answer:** A

**Explanation:** Option A should be chosen as the correct answer because providing a detailed rubric helps students comprehend the specific expectations and objectives for each section of the project. It offers clear guidelines and criteria for success, enabling students to focus their efforts and ensure that their work aligns with the desired outcomes. The other options touch on important aspects of group projects but do not directly address the role of a detailed rubric in guiding students' understanding of the project requirements.

## QUESTION 209

**Answer:** B

**Explanation:** Option B is the correct answer because emphasizing the use of credible and authoritative sources promotes students' research skills by enhancing their ability to evaluate and critically analyze different sources. It encourages them to assess the reliability, validity, and relevance of sources, which is essential for conducting thorough and well-supported research. The other options touch on valuable aspects of research but do not directly address the role of using credible sources in developing research skills.

## QUESTION 210

**Answer:** B

**Explanation:** Option B should be chosen as the correct answer because introducing close reading and providing a short story for analysis helps students develop their literary analysis skills by enhancing their ability to identify and analyze literary devices employed by the author. Close reading encourages students to pay attention to the author's choices, such as symbolism, figurative language, and narrative techniques, which deepens their understanding of the text and its broader literary elements. The other options touch on important aspects of literary analysis but do not directly address the focus on identifying and analyzing literary devices.

## QUESTION 211

**Answer:** D

**Explanation:** High school English teachers should teach students to organize persuasive writing logically or by importance to enhance the effectiveness of their arguments, as described in option D.

## QUESTION 212

**Answer:** C

**Explanation:** The most effective strategy for introducing a topic and developing it thoroughly in an informational or explanatory text is to select and present the most significant and relevant facts, examples, or information. This approach ensures that the content is focused, informative, and engaging for the reader. Personal anecdotes may be useful in some contexts, but they should be used sparingly and only if they directly support the topic. Providing a concise summary without elaboration does not provide sufficient depth or detail. Using abstract concepts and theoretical frameworks may be appropriate in certain scholarly or specialized texts, but it may not be suitable for all audiences or purposes. Therefore, Option C is the correct answer as it emphasizes the importance of selecting and presenting the most relevant and significant information.

## QUESTION 213

**Answer:** B

**Explanation:** Pathos is an appeal to the emotions of the audience. It seeks to evoke feelings, such as empathy, sympathy, joy, anger, or sadness, to sway the audience's opinion or motivate them to take action.

## QUESTION 214

**Answer:** C

**Explanation:** Acknowledging and addressing counterarguments is crucial in persuasive writing because it demonstrates the strength of your argument by refuting opposing viewpoints, as illustrated in option C.

## QUESTION 215

**Answer:** D

**Explanation:** Effective organizational approaches in persuasive writing often involve a clear structure with an introduction, body, and conclusion, as demonstrated in option D.

## QUESTION 216

**Answer:** A

**Explanation:** Option A is the correct answer because incorporating multimedia elements, such as visuals and audio clips, into the presentation contributes to students' presentation skills by engaging the audience and enhancing their understanding of the speech's historical context. Visual aids and audio clips can provide visual and auditory support, helping the audience grasp the significance and impact of the speech within its historical backdrop. The other options touch on valuable aspects of presentations but do not directly address the use of multimedia elements to enhance understanding of the speech's historical context.